HOW TO GET NOTICED BY THE NATIONAL MEDIA:

Your Complete Guide To High-Impact Publicity

Trellis Publishing, Inc.
P.O. Box 16141
Duluth, MN 55816
800-513-0115

How to Get Noticed By the National Media:
Your Complete Guide to High-Impact Publicity

© 2001 text by Jeff Lewis and Dick Jones

Publishers Cataloging-in Publication
(Provided by Quality Books, Inc.)

Lewis, Jeff , 1952-
    How to get noticed by the national media: your complete guide to high-impact
publicity / by Jeff Lewis and Dick Jones. 1st ed.
    p.cm.
    LCCN: 00-112025
    ISBN:1-930650-42-6

    1. Publicity. 2. Mass media and publicity.
    I. Jones, Dick, 1948- II. Title

HD59.L49 2001   659
                         QB100-1095

Cover Design: George Foster, Foster and Foster, 800-472-3953
Book Design: Gary Kruchowski (2001 National Council for Marketing and Public Relations, District V, Communicator of the Year)

To Phyllis, my children and parents. Thank you.
Jeff Lewis

To Ann for all her love and patience.
Dick Jones

Table of Contents

Foreword

Dick Jones and Jeff Lewis have written a book that holds great value for those of us who deal regularly, or even occasionally, with the national media. They know the rules of the game. Jones and Lewis understand the value of hard work and perseverance. They focus their client, consciously shape an image, and appreciate the intersection among public policy, the show business quality of media, and the need to get a message out. This book is a must read for anyone seeking to learn how to represent themselves or their organization to a broader constituency. The authors should be congratulated for providing an interesting, readable and insightful text on how to get the job done and, perhaps even more important, how to know when you succeeded in doing so.

Brian C. Mitchell
President
Washington & Jefferson College

HOW TO GET NOTICED BY THE NATIONAL MEDIA:

Your Complete Guide To High-Impact Publicity

By

Jeff Lewis and Dick Jones

Preface

Attaining national publicity is often viewed as an elusive concept reserved for the rich, famous or infamous. Others believe that trying to garner national publicity tends to distract from the "nuts and bolts" of the tasks at hand. After all, there are local press releases to be written, photo shoots to be arranged, committee meetings to attend, reports to be compiled, ad campaigns to develop, and a variety of damage control priorities. Who has time for a national media campaign?

If by chance a national reporter happens to call an institution or company without being previously solicited, many public relations directors are simply too busy to devote the time and energy necessary to ensure a positive placement. "Things will take care of themselves" they reason, and they hope the reporter will be kind to their organization. But in reality the reporter may not call back. Your organization's shot at 15 minutes of fame has been lost forever.

To some extent, most CEOs in both the corporate and nonprofit sectors crave high profile publicity. Certainly, almost all leaders like to see their institution portrayed in a positive light by the national media. As a result, they often turn to outside consultants who deal exclusively with the national media. Executives and administrators want to rub elbows with the likes of Larry King or Jane Pauley because they know it can benefit their organization, and they will devote some portions of their budgets to ensure results.

This desire for national publicity often results from competitors first attaining placements in the major newspapers or magazines. All of a sudden, your CEO or president is asking you tough questions: "Why can't *The New York Times* run a story about us? How can we get national attention?"

For those in the public relations field who actively seek national publicity for their clients, the continual frustrations and refusals are often too much to bear. The seemingly constant negative reactions or lack of responses from the national media can wear down even the most seasoned public relations pro. After awhile, the communications manager gives up. Being mentioned in *USA Today* doesn't seem to be worth the effort.

There are many who simply contend that their organization has nothing newsworthy at the national level. They mistakenly believe that a corporation, nonprofit organization or college has to be nationally known before the national reporters take them seriously – much like the chicken and egg scenario.

Still others take a jaundiced view of the national media in general. These public relations people believe that any placements connected with such news outlets as *The New York Times, Newsweek* or CNN are beyond their control, and more often than not will result in negative experiences for their institution or company.

"We can get some very good hometown coverage from our local newspapers and TV stations," they contend, "but national media sources always put a negative slant on stories. *U.S. News & World Report* doesn't want to hear from us. They seek out their own story ideas without our help."

You'd be surprised at how often national publications and national broadcast networks depend on a good tip from an insider to develop a story. The trick is knowing what constitutes a good story, and then knowing what to do with it. There are steps that can be taken to increase your odds of scoring with the national media. And oddly enough, these are not arcane methods derived from some secret public relations formula.

On the contrary, most national media placement specialists use common sense and initiative to land that treasured placement in *The New York Times* or *USA Today*, or to schedule that interview with ABC World News Tonight or C-SPAN. There may be some strategies contained in this book that are foreign to you, but many fall under the heading of common sense and good news judgment.

You will learn that time, patience, and resolve are key factors in any national media relations campaign. It is rare indeed to land a placement in *The Washington Post* at the very onset of a national media relations effort. It will take time, perhaps even more time than you can devote to the task.

You will discover through reading this book that the national media are indeed approachable with good story ideas, despite their hurried schedule and lack of tolerance for overzealous public relations (PR) people. You'll find that it is possible to have lunch with a *Wall Street Journal* reporter for the purpose of pitching a story idea. Most national media people are looking for a good story, and you may have it.

More important perhaps than one's knowledge of the public relations business is the methodology employed when seeking national publicity. This always involves a heavy time commitment. The main problem associated with attaining national press is usually not a lack of talent within the PR office, nor a dearth of ideas, but simply not enough time to devote to the task. There's no doubt that perseverance goes a long way when trying to land that elusive placement in *USA Today.*

With the exception of some large companies or major research institutions, the public relations staffs at most companies and nonprofits are too small to maintain consistent high-impact programs. Also, most low-impact activities (such as the announcement of appointments and promotions or news releases on upcoming seminars) are necessary. Regrettably, they don't set your organization apart from the rest.

What will set you apart is national publicity. And it will do so in a way unlike any other. That first national placement will become a milestone in your career and will probably be a moment you'll never forget. The thrill associated with national placements never gets old.

This book will explain step-by-step methods of attaining national publicity, whether you work for a small, rural college or a Fortune 500 company. You will learn the ins and outs of a national media campaign along with the secrets of having the opinions of those in your organization voiced without fear of misquotes or words taken out of context.

In the end, you will become energized and excited about beginning your own quest for national coverage. You will develop a sense of confidence about what it takes to break into the national spotlight, and you will discover why it's worth all the effort for those few shining moments in the sun.

Jeff Lewis

Chapter
One

The Most Commonly Asked Questions
of a National Media Consultant

Q: Why should my company or institution try for major visibility?

A: Major media attention separates you from the pack. In fact, it's a quick way to become distinctive. It shows that your organization is important and worthy of support. It generates a true feeling of respect among your peers. Benefactors give to nonprofits that are seen as winners, students attend colleges that are in the national news, and shareholders and major customers take notice. Also, a third-party endorsement via a national newspaper or broadcast feature of quality and impact shows your organization is a "player" and can add credibility to your organization. Furthermore, national publicity – especially through newspapers – can be leveraged into additional visibility since assignment editors at broadcast outlets often turn to the print media for story ideas.

Q: Can a small organization achieve big recognition?

A: Certainly. The national and major regional media are interested in one thing – a good story. Are you worried that you don't have as many strong stories as Yale, the Carnegie Foundation or Microsoft? So what? That's no reason not to use the ones you have.

Q: What role should I expect media relations to play in a marketing plan?

A: Media visibility is excellent at highlighting an organization's importance. Nothing – neither publications nor advertising – can do it as well. News coverage is valuable for internal and local audiences, but it really pays off with those who are not regularly in touch with your institution. Most organizations need better contact with external audiences; many are not using media relations the right way.

Q: How does an organization misuse media relations?

A: Some expect it to replace advertising. Stories about upcoming events should supplement ads, not replace them. If you depend entirely on news coverage to publicize events or product and program changes, be prepared for disappointments. Your agenda is not necessarily the media's agenda.

Q: Are there other media relations mistakes that corporations and non-profits make?

A: Yes. Some try to give a complete picture of their organization in each release they write. Every story cannot be a history lesson, annual report or catalog. Remember, news organizations are looking for news.

Q: Any other complaints?

A: Yes. Public relations directors frequently take media relations for granted. The time required to carry out an effective media relations plan is significant. It takes as much planning and attention to detail as a major fund drive or a national advertising campaign.

Q: Can media relations replace publications, websites or advertising?

A: No. Publications, websites, advertising, targeted mailings and per-
     sonal contacts are all necessary and valuable. What media visibility
     does so well is highlight the organization in a way that complements
     these activities. When you try for national media visibility, you are
     competing in a much smaller field.

Q: How so?

A: Most corporations and nonprofits produce publications showing
     caring staff and worthy causes. Many use advertising to create inter-
     est and measure response for selected programs and products. But
     you can count on your fingers and toes the number of companies
     that use media relations effectively. A good media relations program
     slices through the marketing "noise."

Q: How do you know if you have enough stories to try for national visi-
     bility?

A: One good story can get you started. Look for material in several
     places. You'll be surprised at what you find. A few unique staff
     members may be feature material. There's probably a story or two
     in your traditions. Important or famous visitors make good stories.
     In-house expertise can be used to plug into breaking news or for
     special seasonal stories. National trends always make news. Where
     does your organization fit in? CEOs, presidents, and key employees
     have opinions on important subjects and the opposite/editorial
     (op/ed) pages are good outlets. And if you work for a college, don't
     forget – even though yours may not be a research institution, there
     may be newsworthy scholarship being conducted in a few places.

Q: How long does an effective national media relations campaign take
     to implement?

A: Much depends on the desired outcomes. Distinct campaigns for varied clientele differ in time and scope. However, not too much should be expected during the first three months of any national plan. It takes at least that amount of time to shape the plan into working order. Contacts must be established through personal calls, and media lists must be updated for specific markets. Your first national placement may not be attained until six months into the campaign. Or you may strike gold early in the process. It is hard to predict when success will come.

Q: How can you maximize the benefits of major visibility?

A: Reprints of articles and transcripts of broadcasts are extremely useful for political purposes. They also lend credibility to internal publications. The fact that your organization receives national exposure can be cited in your brochures and pamphlets. And the same materials used to gain major visibility can also be employed with great success locally. Your hometown coverage improves too, as the local media come to understand that they have a nationally recognized player in town.

Q: Can an organization achieve high-impact public relations without the cooperation of the CEO or president?

A: Not likely. Apart from needing the necessary budgetary increases for costs in your plan, such as consultant fees, travel expenses to New York and Washington, DC, or even additional phone calls and faxes to the national media, there's the issue of access. A portion of the story ideas that you'll be pitching to the national media may involve some aspect of the person in charge. Take this away and you immediately lose a great weapon.

Q: Is it possible to implement a high-impact media campaign without the use of a consultant?

A: Absolutely. With the help of this book and a commitment to the task at hand, most public relations directors can attain national visibility for their organization or company. But be prepared to devote a considerable amount of time to the cause. You can estimate that you'll need to spend at least 20 percent of the average workweek over the course of several months in order to have a fighting chance with the national press.

Q: What about national media consultant firms? How do they achieve a high degree of success with the appropriate news outlets?

A: Time and contacts. Simply put, these firms and individuals devote 100 percent of their time towards establishing contacts and pitching stories. Their efforts help build a rapport with the national media. Their success rate may only be five to ten percent, but that rate translates into huge results for the client. Without the proper time commitment – often 20 hours per week on one account directed at a few national outlets – you are destined for problems. Always expect the unexpected when dealing with the national media. For instance, your fax never reached the reporter's desk. Your voice mail message was inadvertently erased. The assignment editor never received your media package. You spend much time redoing tasks you've already done, but that is the nature of the business, and with practice you'll learn to persevere until you get your break.

Q: If I sign a contract with a consultant firm, what type of contract should I expect?

A: It varies, but many of the specialized firms work on a yearly retainer in order to maximize the yield of the contract. In other words, these consultants need time to garner results because of the nature of the business and therefore they are leery of short-term contracts. Fees can range from $19,000 per year to $65,000 depending on the breadth of the contract. For example, some national media relations firms will offer their clients monthly tip sheets detailing reporter coverage and outlining various topics of interest by the national media. In this type of contract, the actual placement process is left up to the client's public relations manager. At the other end of the spectrum is the "inclusive" contract, which covers everything from conception to placement. However, there are firms who conduct business via a placement-by-placement fee. For example, a feature in *The New York Times* might be worth $5,000. A mention in *USA Today* might cost $1,500. This way of doing business is frowned upon by most people in the public relations business because it goes against the Public Relations Society of America (PRSA) code of ethics. Putting a price tag on specific placements raises many concerns, perhaps most notable being a perception by the client that one will ignore perfectly legitimate news outlets in a unrealistic quest for the Holy Grail - *The New York Times*, CNN, or *Time Magazine*. In addition, even the best public relations professional cannot control to any great degree the amount and/or nature of various placements. Thus, it is possible to work diligently on a project for months and not attain a significant placement. The vast majority of public relations consultants and companies work on a yearly retainer, regardless of the results. With a reputable public relations firm or consultant, the results will vary over the course of the year, but there will be results eventually.

Q: What are some of the parameters for judging the success of a national media campaign?

A: You must begin with realistic expectations. Goals and objectives should be developed before embarking on any campaign. You may want to engage the advice of a consultant at an early stage simply to ascertain what is realistic for you compared to what your competition is doing. Of course, all national media campaigns differ slightly. Texas A&M University certainly expects more national coverage than does Claremont McKenna College because Texas A&M is a much larger institution with more research and faculty to promote. A national feature, several mentions, two op/ed placements and a network talk show interview within a year's time would be deemed very successful. A slight downward variation would be acceptable.

Q: Please explain in detail the ideal client/consultant relationship.

A: There can be varied degrees of trepidation on the part of some public relations departments concerning a contract with a national media relations consultant. For example, if the president or CEO brought in the consultant, there's a natural tendency for the public relations director to feel threatened. "Why," he or she may wonder, "do we need an outside public relations consultant? That's what I'm here for." It's a fair question, to be sure, but one that can be dealt with in a very diplomatic manner. In fact, it's a common concern among public relations department personnel if they were not the ones to bring in the consultant.

We find that the decision to hire our services normally begins with the public relations director who may have heard us speak at a seminar or may have come across our names via word of mouth from colleagues. When that is the case, our professional relationship with that office almost always gets off to a good start. After all, the PR director personally requested our services. And they may have needed to justify our services and fees with the president or CEO. A strong relationship can develop quickly.

On the other hand, if the president or CEO called us in, (especially without advising the public relations department within his or her organization) then perhaps some fears need to be assuaged. It is never our goal to replace or lessen the responsibilities of the public relations director. And quite frankly, this has never happened during our time in the business. We merely serve as an extension of the public relations department. With the exception of a few selected employees within the company or university whom we interview for media placement purposes, no one knows we exist. We like it that way. Once the national recognition begins to materialize for the organization, the public relations department is the one that receives the praise and accolades. We like it that way, too.

Our relationship with the public relations department most often develops into a healthy, reciprocated feeling of respect. We understand that they are normally far too busy to concentrate on a national media relations plan. And they understand that we aren't there to impose our will or to intrude where we don't belong.

Are there degrees of partnerships with one another? Absolutely. It's not uncommon for personal friendships to develop, and we continue to exchange holiday cards, including personal notes and updates, with quite a few of our clients from the past. The beauty of the relationship lies in the ability to take the department to new heights by attaining national publicity. When that happens, everyone is content.

Chapter

TWO

What National Publicity Can Do For You

By definition, media relations is a process by which trained personnel, usually with a public relations or journalism background, attempt to gain positive exposure for their company or organization. This exposure can come in many forms but it often aligns itself to placements in the print and broadcast media.

The media relations area specifically involves the promotional activities of an organization. It includes press releases, feature stories, advertising, and arranging photo shoots. The public relations director normally has a degree in public relations, journalism, or sometimes English. Strong writing skills are especially important. A newspaper background is often helpful since it's good to know which stories can be successfully pitched to the print or broadcast media, and being a former reporter gives valuable insight into how an assignment editor or city editor thinks.

Where does national media relations fit into your organization's marketing plan? You should ask yourself that question because your bosses certainly will ask it of you.

The short answer is that media relations work is an element of marketing. It helps with "positioning" tasks such as name recognition and product "branding." National media attention is also a third-party endorsement of quality and importance. This endorsement, usually aimed at an outside audience, also resonates within the company.

"You have no idea what this will do for us," said an official of a small high-tech research and development firm when told that his company would be the subject of an article in *The Wall Street Journal.* "Our employees really need this kind of encouragement." The firm had been working for ten years to bring an important technology to market.

Recognition in *The Journal*, while intended to help market the product, also had the effect of validating all the years of hard work by those inside the firm. "Unlike paid advertising, media coverage has public credibility, offering a potential boost to a marketing effort, an aid in negotiations with customers and suppliers, and a public pat on the back for employees," said *INC. Magazine* writer Curtis Hartman in an April 1988 article on national media relations.

Media relations work is not separate from marketing. It is a part of marketing. In the last 20 years there has been much wheel spinning over the alleged differences between marketing and public relations and between public relations and advertising. Our view is that media relations work is a part of public relations. Advertising is another separate part of public relations.

The Jones/Lewis National Media Relations Chart

Public relations is a part of the overall marketing effort that includes your organization's products, their price(s), the places and ways your products and services reach your customers, and the promotional efforts you employ to call these elements to the attention of your customers.

Public relations – of which national media relations is one element – is growing in emphasis in the marketing mix. Asked to rank marketing tactics in order of importance, senior executives now rank public relations ahead of advertising, according to a study by the American Advertising Federation reported in the July 26, 1999 issue of *Business Week*. Product Development was at the top, followed in order by strategic planning, public relations, research and development, financial strategies, advertising, and legal.

For nonprofits, successful national media relations can help with the critical prestige factor so necessary to conduct fund raising campaigns and secure members or enrollees. Roger Williams and Robert Hendrickson wrote in their 1986 article for the Association of Governing Boards (AGB) Reports that "The most important factor for fund-raising success is institutional prestige." Among nonprofits, colleges and universities have grasped this truth most clearly.

"Foundations have much to learn from the best work done on campuses," writes Ronald Gross, formerly with the Ford Foundation, in *The Chronicle of Philanthropy.* "Twenty-five years ago colleges and universities were generally disregardful, if not suspicious, of the press. Faculty members and administrators generally operated on the assumption that no news was good news. The public information function was peripheral and feeble.

Today virtually all colleges and universities strive to share their expertise. In philanthropy, however, the attitude still prevails that if one's expertise might be useful, the press will seek it out. Unfortunately, it doesn't work that way. Pressures on the press preclude it. Reporters, editors and others need help in gaining access to foundation expertise – indeed in knowing that it is there."

Everyone needs to embrace this lesson, not just philanthropies. Museums, charitable organizations, government and social service units all have expertise to share that should be of interest to the public if it can be communicated to them through the news media. And by sharing that expertise, prestige accrues to the organization.

As we consult with various institutions throughout the country, the first image conjured up by the term "public relations" is free publicity. After all, these organizations usually have within their structure separate budgets and departments for advertising, public affairs, governmental relations, photography and special events.

It is the positive newspaper feature or favorable broadcast sound bite about their institution that they are seeking from public relations – and for good reason. A 1,000-word article on the merits of their organization in *The New York Times* is obviously much more cost effective (when you take into account a consultant's fee versus paid advertising) and usually carries with it far more credibility than does a full-page, $40,000 ad. The public often views certain advertising campaigns with a jaundiced eye and will either glance over ads or ridicule them for their lack of creativity and honesty.

There's little doubt that highly sophisticated advertising campaigns can produce desired results for an organization if created properly. But at what cost to an organization? Market research tells us that many ads do indeed increase the sales productivity at all levels throughout a company. However, are the public relations pros trying to sell a product, an idea, or a message?

Therein lies the dilemma faced by many of us in the **PR** profession. If you are selling toothpaste, perhaps advertising is the way to go. On the other hand, trying to convince the public about the merits of an organizational philosophy takes a learned public relations pro. It's rare for an advertising campaign, no matter how substantial the budget, to effectively promote the philosophy behind its sponsor.

Of course, there are exceptions to this rule. Nike's "Just Do It" or Saturn's "Same Price for All Cars" captures a company's philosophy, but not as in-depth as would a national media relations campaign that includes features on the **CEO** and op/eds.

A plan that works for McDonalds will not necessarily work for another Fortune 500 company. Surely, such a plan will not work for the Ford Foundation. The missions of the two are not similar. As such, there needs to be different approaches to national exposure.

Most **PR** people are not employed to sell hamburgers. We leave that to our colleagues in advertising. As national media relations consultants, we are often trying to get out a message that explains the philosophy behind an organization, company, nonprofit or university. That message may help to sell a product or increase admissions but it does so in a way that also enhances the image of the client and the self-image of those who identify with the client.

The following excerpt from an article we placed in *The Wall Street Journal* demonstrates this point.

"It's Unlikely Holders Of This Sheepskin Will Act Like Sheep"
by Gary Putka
The Wall Street Journal, Nov. 12, 1992

Matt Zemon wants to lead. "I've just always been a leader," says Mr. Zemon, a junior at the University of Richmond. Amy Averill wants to lead, too. If all goes well, Mr. Zemon and Ms. Averill will graduate in 1994 with bachelors' degrees in leadership studies. Not leadership of anything in particular – just leadership.

The courses are part of the Jepson School of Leadership Studies, a new and well-funded effort to teach people how to lead. A boom in research and writing about leadership – and a $20 million gift from businessman alumnus Robert Jepson – has convinced the University of Richmond that leadership should be taught.

Public relations is a much more subtle approach than advertising. It strives to create a favorable climate in which an organization can flourish. Public relations and communications directors sit behind their computers writing press releases, arranging photo shoots for a check-passing ceremony, and working on speeches for the president. The communications business, we often discover, is not one of glamour and intrigue. It is not an area where the creative writing courses we took in college normally have as much effect as we might wish.

Instead, we find ourselves searching each day for the five "Ws" of the story and converting this knowledge into the inverted pyramid style. How we long for a story with an hourglass format and narrative prose as opposed to the summary lead.

This all changes when preparing a national media relations plan. Writing pitch letters that get noticed by national reporters surely takes skill and creativity. In some ways this can be equated to writing advertising copy for a billboard campaign. With billboards, you only have eight to ten words to make your point. Similarly, the first few words of a pitch letter will make or break you.

You have ten seconds to show a journalist that you have a story of interest. No, make it seven seconds. If you haven't hooked them right away, you probably won't. Leads are important. People with degrees in public relations – but with no journalism experience – are often dismayed when good PR jobs go to former journalists. One of the reasons this happens is that journalists tend to know how to write good leads.

Good leads sell good stories – and sometimes merely adequate stories. And bad leads can sink stories that should have been easy sells. The lead has two purposes: first, to hook media gatekeepers and convince them that what you have to say is worth the time it will take them to read it, or in the case of a phone pitch, to listen to it; second, to move them on to the next bit of information you want to impart.

Sometimes you can accomplish these objectives by writing something clever. It's hard to be clever, however, and attempts to be cute often don't succeed. More often, you can do the job by writing something short and to the point.

"The lead," said Rene J. Cappon, "should have maximum effect with minimum of phrase. Think of (leads) as if they cost you ten bucks per word, each word to be engraved on stainless steel while you are sitting on a hot stove. Think economy."

Here are some examples of leads from the worlds of journalism and public relations. Remember, you only have a very limited time frame in which to capture the interest of the national reporter.

"The President was shot in a theater tonight and perhaps mortally wounded." This lead, by Lawrence Gobright of the *Associated Press* was filed on April 14, 1865 and was used by Rene Cappon in his classic guide, "The Word: An Associated Press Guide to Good News Writing". It's a perfect model for the saying, "use a small lead for a big story." To put this in a media relations context, if your firm's research and development department has found a cure for the common cold, all you have to do is say so.

"Pennsylvania's bees are feeling the sting of a hard winter." One function of a lead is to give a capsule summary of the story. Another is to move the reader to the second paragraph. What happened to these bees?

"Leadership can be taught. That's the premise of the new Jepson School of Leadership Studies at the University of Richmond." This is a summary lead that answers the "what" and "where" questions.

"A device that mimics the human eye with far greater speed and precision than anything ever invented will be offered to prospective buyers early in the year 2000 in what is believed to be the world's first-ever high technology auction." This lead, faxed to a reporter at *The Wall Street Journal* in the morning, yielded a callback in the afternoon. *The Journal* did the story. The letter was three pages long but everything the journalist needed to know to make a "yes" or "no" decision was in that first sentence.

"Baseball players at Mansfield University must do three things well: field, hit and baby-sit." This was a story about how the baseball team entertained children in the gym while their parents went Christmas shopping. The goal was to raise money for a spring-training trip to Florida. *Sports Illustrated* did the story.

"What organizers believe to be the largest maze in the world is being built in a cornfield adjacent to Lebanon Valley College in Annville, PA." When a producer for "Good Morning America" read this letter she wrote "book this" right on it.

Yes, we all know it is easier to sell a story if it has elements such as being the "world's first" or the "world's largest." Most of our stories, of course, are more prosaic.

"Administrators at Texas Christian University wanted to keep more juniors and seniors on campus. So they gave them what they were going off campus to find: affordable apartment-style living." Not flashy, this summary lead gives journalists enough information to make a decision about whether to proceed to paragraph number two. It resulted in a national *Associated Press* wire story.

Don't bury the lead. It is the most common mistake made by journalists and public relations practitioners. Many writers, perhaps most, spend too much time "clearing their throat." That is, they set the stage, give the background, dole out some pats on the back to the company president, mention the firm's pioneering role in widget technology, and finally, about the fourth or fifth paragraph, get around to making their point. Too late. That letter is already in the wastebasket.

Almost everyone in the public relations field took an introductory news writing class in college. On the first or second day of that class, they learned about the "inverted pyramid," the idea that in journalistic-style writing you put the important points up front. The supporting information, in descending order of value, follows. In retrospect, that adage – delivered early in the course and too often forgotten – is one of the most important lessons public relations people can learn about writing effective pitch letters and news releases. With national publicity efforts, the creative juices can sprout forth.

"I have great respect for the public relations person who can generate a national clip for a rural college in Iowa," says John McGauley, president of Gehrung Associates, a national media relations firm in Keene, New Hampshire. "When *The Wall Street Journal* features a Nobel Prize winner from Stanford or simply rewrites a *New England Journal of Medicine* article from a whiz-bang Harvard researcher, that can hardly be attributed to the skill of the PR office. However, when that rural college in Iowa gets national publicity, that takes skill and creativity on someone's part."

National publicity helps an organization become distinctive in its market. It lends a third-party endorsement to the efforts of that organization and shows that it is worthy of support. Benefactors give to schools or foundations that are seen as winners. And students attend those institutions of higher learning.

Those in the corporate sector experience benefits of their own. National publicity can often create a positive surge in image and ultimately sales and profits. Moreover, it creates respect among your competitors. For example, a CEO being profiled in *Fortune* as a hands-on, results-oriented individual can often leave the competition groping for answers as far as corporate identity is concerned.

Of course, the message is far more important than the messenger. Developing talking points for a college president or CEO is imperative. You'll read more about that in later chapters. Most organizations have a story to tell. As a result, national media relations counselors have one clear message ingrained in their psyche as they travel the country representing all sorts of nonprofits and companies; every campus or boardroom has a news peg to polish or a promotion to pitch.

Granted, not all institutions are created equal. But it's the job of all public relations directors to find, develop and then create the impression that a particular story is too interesting to be passed over by the national news. A national clip immediately does several things for an organization: first, it has a great impact internally by generating a real sense of pride among employees and staff; second, it has the benefit of awarding immediate legitimacy to external constituencies such as customers, board members, and stockholders.

"People on campus actually seem to stand up and walk straighter after a national article," one college president notes. At Marywood University in Scranton, Pennsylvania, students reported that several national articles made them proudly bring the Marywood sweatshirt out of the closet. Quite frankly, steering committees at nonprofits enjoy the prestige, as do stockholders of small and large companies.

The Amazing Maize Maze in Lancaster, Pennsylvania experienced a surge in visits from people throughout the country as the result of features in *The New York Times, Washington Post,* and *National Geographic.* Created by Disney co-producer Don Frantz, the Maze's strategy was to use limited advertising dollars, but instead concentrate heavily on a national media relations campaign. The national results pleased Frantz so much that national media relations became the focal point for his annual corn project.

Getting the name of your organization in a national publication also sends a clear message to the competition. In effect, it says that your company or nonprofit is on the cutting edge. It reinforces the quality of work being conducted and often highlights subtle details of an organization that heretofore have gone unnoticed by your peers and colleagues.

The term "national media" usually refers to *The New York Times, Wall Street Journal, Washington Post, USA Today* and *Los Angeles Times.* These are the newspapers that are circulated in most major cities throughout the country. A person can go to a newsstand in Bozeman, Montana and pick up a copy of one of these publications. Of course, all of the major news magazines carry a similar distinction, as do the major television outlets. Don't forget CNN and C-SPAN.

But as far as newspapers are concerned, it's the New York, Washington, D.C. or Los Angeles-based publications that are generally considered national in scope. Major metropolitan newspapers such as the *Chicago Tribune, Boston Globe* and *Dallas Morning News* are also extremely important news outlets with which public relations people need to stay in contact. Actually, it's often much harder to crack these papers since they tend to be provincial by nature.

But don't forget, there are literally hundreds of media outlets out there. Paul Harvey reaches 33 million listeners each week on the ABC Radio Network.

The list of high circulation magazines may surprise even some veteran public relations people, but there are numerous publications that surpass one million in circulation. This, of course, translates into vast numbers of readers using the "2.7 reader x circulation" formula.

Table A: Magazine Circulation	
Publication	Circulation
Modern Maturity	20,500,000
Reader's Digest	15,400,000
TV Guide	13,300,000
National Geographic	8,898,000
Better Homes & Gardens	7,800,000
Good Housekeeping	7,560,000
The Cable Guide	6,800,000
Family Circle	5,635,000
Consumer's Report	5,000,000
Ladies' Home Journal	4,700,000
McCall's	4,350,000
Time	4,315,000
Woman's Day	4,250,000
People	3,800,000
Prevention	3,491,000
Sports Illustrated	3,419,000
Playboy	3,400,000
Car & Travel	3,376,000
Newsweek	3,330,000
Home & Away	3,070,000
Redbook	2,930,000
The American Legion Magazine	2,700,000
Cosmopolitan	2,625,000
Seventeen	2,550,000
Martha Stewart Living	2,506,000
Star	2,500,000

Southern Living	2,490,000
YM	2,315,000
Glamour	2,270,000
National Enquirer	2,250,000
Smithsonian	2,150,000
U.S. News & World Report	2,110,000
VFW Magazine	2,100,000
Money	2,070,000
Teen	1,905,000
Ebony	1,850,000
Parents	1,840,000
Field & Stream	1,820,000
Country Living	1,720,000
Men's Health	1,700,000
Life	1,646,000
Popular Science	1,605,000
Golf Digest	1,575,000
Woman's World	1,555,000
Sunset	1,545,000
First for Women	1,500,000
Popular Mechanics	1,460,000
Entertainment Weekly	1,452,000
Cooking Light	1,420,000
Outdoor Life	1,414,000
Golf Magazine	1,380,000
American Rifleman	1,350,000
Rolling Stone	1,300,000
Boy's Life	1,295,000
Discover	1,260,000
New Woman	1,260,000
Weight Watchers Magazine	1,250,000
Mademoiselle	1,250,000
Car & Driver	1,249,000
PC World	1,239,000
PC Magazine	1,230,000
Elks Magazine	1,200,000
Self	1,200,000
Family Handyman	1,185,000

Endless Vacation 1,180,000
Vogue 1,165,000
Kiplinger's Personal Finance 1,150,000
Sesame Street Magazine 1,150,000
Soap Opera Digest 1,145,000
Vanity Fair 1,145,000
US 1,135,000
Essence 1,100,000
Scouting 1,088,000
Bon Appetite 1,085,000
Country Home 1,065,000
Home 1,060,000
Penthouse 1,005,000

(Source: THE GEBBE PRESS "ALL IN ONE" DIRECTORY, COPYRIGHT 2000)

There are scores of other national magazines whose circulation falls under the one million mark, but whose attention may be far more important to your client's cause. For example, *The Atlantic Monthly* reports a paid circulation of just under 500,000, surely a substantial number. More important, however, is its impact on the intellectual world.

When one of our clients, the Annenberg Washington Program in Washington, D.C., received a substantial placement in *The Atlantic Monthly*, the program became nationally known almost overnight, despite the fact that it had been conducting quality research for years before the feature article. With just one placement, the program gained acceptance in the minds of other think tanks and journalists who cover such topics at the national level.

This author remembers calling an assignment editor at C-SPAN shortly after the article in *The Atlantic Monthly* ran. The editor immediately referenced the fact that she had seen the article and that she found it to be very interesting. That article opened the door for further conversation, which eventually led to C-SPAN coming to cover the next event at Annenberg.

Would this have happened had the assignment editor not seen the feature in *The Atlantic Monthly*? Hard to say, but our guess is probably not. The article immediately increased the program's importance in the mind of the media. There's little doubt this happens on a regular basis.

Are we advocating that national media relations means trying to place an article in each of the widely circulated publications? Not at all. There are obvious reasons why many of the magazines, perhaps a majority, would not be suitable for your national media relations plans. However, don't ignore them.

From a development perspective, most officials at colleges and other nonprofits say their fund-raising efforts are usually affected positively by national publicity through an increase in donations from people who experience a greater "kindred spirit" to the nonprofit. Communications theory tells us that positive media attention reinforces good feelings among those who already think well of an organization. Because of this, many development directors employ the services of national media consultants prior to beginning the public phase of a capital campaign.

The object of gaining national attention before any fund-raising effort is akin to a surge in advertising prior to a political campaign. It seems that those who have the name recognition are usually the ones who are successful. Take, for example, the College of William and Mary, a prestigious institution of higher learning and second oldest college in the country (behind only Harvard.)

Situated on a gem of a campus in Williamsburg, Va., the College of William and Mary is certainly blessed with a loyal alumni constituency. Nevertheless, before embarking on the largest capital campaign in the school's 300-year history, then president Paul Verkuil decided that a number of high-profile articles would help the cause.

We had to determine the focus of the national media campaign. Sure, any positive national publicity is normally good news for the client. But in this case, spreading the college too thin with a number of small and disconnected stories would detract from the overall purpose – to let William and Mary's alumni throughout the country recognize the need to contribute to the capital campaign.

The focus would have to be President Verkuil himself. A number of interviews with national reporters and ensuing articles helped to invigorate the campaign, especially among those alumni who had not seen the college's name in print for a while. President Verkuil himself was quite adept at making a strong case for additional funding to help bolster the overall campaign. In fact, a mention of the campaign in a front page *Sunday New York Times* article greatly enhanced the cause.

President Verkuil also made himself available to the national broadcast media. He knew that any national publicity he could garner would be beneficial as he traveled the country asking alumni to contribute to the fund raising campaign. His philosophy was, "I'll do anything it takes to help William and Mary reach its goal."

One of his assignments happened to be an appearance on "Good Morning America." Ironically, when I first pitched the story idea to the producers of "Good Morning America," it was intended for another one of our clients at the time. The issue of women's studies was a hot topic, and it seemed that a particular college of ours was well suited to discuss their programs in relationship to the topic. The producers liked the concept and wanted to interview the college president the next morning live on "Good Morning America." Sometimes things happen quickly with the broadcast media.

I soon discovered via a call to our client that the college's public relations office was not willing to approach their president with the "Good Morning America" offer. "Too risky," they said. "Our president can't chance it."

"Can't chance what?" I thought. "Can't chance the risk of telling the world all the positive things that are occurring at the college?" I tried to assure them that this was not to be a negative interview, but to no avail. They said they needed weeks of preparation time.

President Verkuil of William and Mary needed only a minute's notice. It so happened that he was on a plane to Los Angeles to meet with some alumni to talk about the capital campaign. We reached him as soon as his plane landed. He agreed to do the "Good Morning America" interview within seconds of hearing of the opportunity. He only needed to know a little about the subject, and we filled him in on the logistics. He needed to be at the Los Angeles studio at 3:30 a.m. the next day. "No problem," he said, even though he just completed a cross-country flight. He understood that this was a unique opportunity to place William and Mary in front of millions of viewers.

In addition, President Verkuil was comfortable with the topic of women's studies since he believed that the college excelled in that area. We prepped him further on the topic, and the interview with "Good Morning America" went very well. President Verkuil, despite the early hour, was relaxed and calm.

The interview went so well, in fact, that quite a few of the prospective donors President Verkuil met with while on the west coast mentioned how much they liked the interview. In the end, the College of William and Mary made their goal. Would they have made the goal without the "Good Morning America" interview? Perhaps, but it surely helped the cause. It's hard to calculate a return on investment for national placements in papers and on broadcast networks, but it's safe to assume that such publicity can assist development efforts.

Apart from benefits for a capital campaign, student inquiries and applications often rise as a direct result of national publicity. Lebanon Valley College in rural Pennsylvania saw applications rise over 25 percent in one year after the school received national ink and airtime about an innovative financial aid package. With continued national publicity, Lebanon Valley's enrollment rose over eight years by an amazing 65 percent and continues on an upward trend to this day.

Furthermore, savvy PR directors can parlay national press into interesting advertising campaigns and admissions packages. In addition, let's not forget the impact national publicity has on some college rankings, especially the subjective "academic reputation" section in the *U.S. News & World Report* issue.

We once asked Robert Morse, deputy director of data research at *U.S. News & World Report* in charge of the "Best Colleges" issue, why one of our new accounts had received a low ranking for academic reputation, and how could they improve. "That's your job," he replied. In other words, get them national publicity and their peers (the other colleges that vote for the academic reputation section) will begin to rank them higher.

Corporate CEOs who have the ability to attract positive national attention, such as Wendy's Dave Thomas, surely add to the attractiveness of their company's image and in turn, tend to keep a more satisfied stable of stockholders. Obviously many corporate CEOs already know this and use their natural rapport with the national media to their advantage.

Bill Glavin, a former top executive with Xerox, is a prime example. Mr. Glavin left the corporate sector to take over as leader of Babson College, a business school near Boston. As president of Babson, Mr. Glavin helped transform a good school into one of the best of its kind in the country.

One of Mr. Glavin's first priorities was to increase the school's national exposure. He led by example. Embarking on an exhaustive national media campaign, Mr. Glavin personally visited New York and Washington, D.C. on numerous occasions in order to promote the positive qualities of Babson.

The ensuing results were impressive: A number of prominent national placements, such as the article excerpted below, bolstered Babson's reputation beyond the borders of Bean Town. A few years later, *U.S. News & World Report* named Babson as the number one small business school in the country. Of course, national publicity wasn't the sole determining factor, but it surely helped the cause.

"New Babson boss, William Glavin, relies on strategic planning: Businesslike Business School"
by Claudia Deutsch
New York Times, 1990

...He has performed a kind of administrative triage. Some decisions he delegates. When the faculty asked him whether they should form a faculty senate, he wouldn't bite. "That's their business," he said. Though Babson's president has always run faculty meetings, he lets the dean of faculty do it.

But for those issues that he feels are within his purview – strategic planning, say, or capital outlay – Mr. Glavin acts decisively. "I always feel that if I present my ideas well I can affect decisions," Mr. Fetters said. "But there's no question that he is the one who makes them and carries them out."

Reprinted from the New York Times, © 1990. All rights reserved.

The Annenberg Washington Program also recognized the value of national publicity. A think tank specializing in communications policy issues, The Annenberg Washington Program needed to distinguish itself from the many other fine programs run under the auspices of legendary philanthropist Walter Annenberg. With a cadre of top-level researchers and Fellows at its disposal, the Annenberg Washington Program had everything going for itself, with the exception of a national media plan. They wanted very badly to let the rest of the country know about their impressive research.

Despite having Newton Minow (former chairman of the Federal Communications Commission) as its director, the Annenberg Program failed to initially attract the kind of national publicity it had expected. A well-constructed national media relations plan began to take effect, including op/eds and media sessions in Washington, DC and New York. The program's name started appearing in a number of national publications.

The results were just what the program needed – recognition as a major player in the communications field. And almost as soon as the program began to see itself in the national news, it also began to experience a greater number of applications for aspiring Fellows.

It is this recognition among colleagues that can spur certain corporate CEOs to invest in a national media consultant. Top CEOs and corporate managers may be making millions of dollars each year in salary, stock options and other perks. Yet many of them crave national attention. And once they've experienced that first flash in the national spotlight, there's usually no stopping them, and they're willing to invest more time toward being involved as an integral part of a strategic national media relations campaign.

Be careful not to let the "ego factor" play too large a role in your national media relations campaign since it's possible your CEO or president may decide to take a similar position with another company somewhere down the road. If so, the support you need for national publicity may go out the door with the departed CEO. Try and garner the support of not only the CEO, but also the entire executive team before implementing a national media relations plan.

Also, if the "ego factor" is your sole purpose for a national media relations campaign, it's likely you won't be able to leverage the national publicity if it happens to come your way. Satisfying the ego of a CEO may not give you the slant in the stories you need to ensure desired results. A good story can be used in a variety of ways: including the clips in the annual report; using the clips as part of an advertising plan; sending tear sheets to Board members and to local media outlets; incorporating the clips in company newsletters. National publicity should become part of the overall marketing campaign. Can it satisfy your CEO's ego as well? Of course, but make certain that your campaign goes well beyond that purpose.

In just about all instances, national publicity strengthens your organization or company by endorsing your mission or product and by expanding your market and influence. It can shake the leaves of your employee tree by arousing in them a sense of pride and purpose. Almost instantaneously, a snowball effect begins and other employees – besides those featured in the original national placement – start to think about projects of their own that may have national publicity potential. We've seen first-hand results that support such a contention.

At Marywood University in Scranton, Pennsylvania the national media relations plan initially began at the top, with Sister Mary Reap, IHM, the president of the university. Sister Mary was a perfect role model for the rest of the university as far as national publicity was concerned. Bright, articulate, and energetic, she accepted the concept with a sense of enthusiasm that became contagious among her staff and student body. Beginning with an op/ed about catholic identity that was syndicated nationally by Scripps Howard News Service, Sister Mary quickly became the "go to" person for several national reporters who covered higher education and/or religion issues.

It wasn't long before several of the faculty at Marywood began to notice the national publicity and wanted to contribute their own expertise and research to the fray. For a period of three years, a number of national articles began appearing in such newspapers and media outlets as *The New York Times, USA Today,* Associated Press, *Wall Street Journal* and *The Washington Post.*

"National publicity certainly brought us a lot of positive name recognition and very good exposure for the university," says Sister Mary. "It also enhanced the pride of internal constituencies and friends, and gave people the opportunity to recognize the particular strengths of the university."

On the surface, it may not appear that the University of California Berkeley would need any help in the area of national publicity. After all, most people consider this fine academic institution to be, along with Stanford, one of the "Ivies" of the west. Their reasons for desiring national attention were quite different from many other clients within the higher education field.

Prior to our services, Berkeley had enjoyed an illustrious reputation as a campus that continually sprouted forth innovative and scholarly research. Hardly a week went by that some mention of Berkeley did not appear in the national news. Berkeley was accustomed to being in the national spotlight. Then why bring on consultants? Officials at Berkeley believed that a pragmatic and purposeful approach to national publicity would result in better control of the type of articles that appeared about the university. Along with the positive publicity at Berkeley came their fair share of negative stories that often cast Berkeley in an unfavorable light. "The land of fruits and nuts," someone once wrote. And Berkeley officials also believed that national media relations consultants from the east coast would be able to work effectively with the major east coast publications and broadcast outlets.

Although no media relations campaign can control periodic articles that tend to disparage a particular university or company, it can offset those stories through a well-constructed national media campaign that gathers a wider variety of consistent placements. For Berkeley, it was agreed that national publicity needed to position the university as one of the finest not only the west, but also in the entire country. That meant using the powerful east coast newspapers to run articles about the faculty and students at Berkeley. This would include not only the mainstream giants but also influential newspapers such as the *Christian Science Monitor*, a newspaper that often helps set the agenda for national news stories, and some very important trade publications.

The details will be outlined in the next chapter, but this example is provided here to underscore another important aspect of national media relations: Attaining national publicity is a wonderful way to expand your market and influence in areas which are important for your mission.

A 'Stranger From a Different Shore' Recounts the Little Known History of Asian Americans
By Carolyn J. Mooney
Chronicle of Higher Education, October 11, 1989

In learning about immigration to the United States, Americans are far more likely to have heard about the pioneers who came west from their assorted old countries than those who came east. To

1

most, the symbolic gateway to this country was Ellis Island, not
Angel Island, the one-time depot in San Francisco Bay where immigrants – primarily from Asia – were processed.

For Ronald Takaki, that fact has served as both painful reminder
and sad comment on how ignorant many people in this country
remain about the cultural ingredients that went into America's melt-
ing pot.

"My family has been here more than 100 years, yet people still ask
me what country I'm from," says Mr. Takaki, a professor of Asian
American studies at the University of California at Berkeley. "Most
people didn't see me as an American," says Mr. Takaki, whose
ancestors came from Japan. "Then I finally realized I was a
stranger from a different shore."

That realization became the focus of a book, "Stangers From a
Different Shore: A History of Asian Americans" (Little, Brown and
Company). In it, Mr. Takaki seeks to give Asian Americans a voice
in American history and to give readers of all backgrounds a fresh
vision of immigration in the United States.

The narrative is a blend of historical background, anecdotes, and
interviews with Asian Americans, richly punctuated with excerpts
from immigrants' letters, verse, and folk-song lyrics. One excerpt
describes a list of commodities a plantation owner requested from a
shipping house in 1890: "bone meal, canvas, Japanese laborers,
macaroni, Chinamen."

Mr. Takaki's book traces the history of Asian Americans by looking
at the diverse experiences of various Asian ethnic groups. He follows the lives of miners, railroad workers, laundrymen, plantation
workers, and boat people, and goes on to show how Asian
Americans have become the fastest growing minority group. They
now represent just over 2 percent of the U.S. population and about
9 percent of California's population, he writes.

Yet, says Mr. Takaki in an interview, "Our universities are not edu-
cating us about our diversity." Why not give students a different perspective of World War II, he asks, by letting them see it from behind
the barbed wires of an internment camp? "That would be a fresh
view," he says.

2

Besides providing that view, Mr. Takaki's book seeks to dispel many myths and sterotypes, such as that of the Chinese laundryman (the Chinese learned the trade in the United States, since there were no laundries in China), as well as to dispel the "model minority" image associated with many Asian Americans today.

Recently, Mr. Takaki saw a film in which Korean greengrocers in New York City were depicted as successful, hard working newcomers to the country. What the film didn't show, he explains, was that many such greengrocers had held professional jobs in their native countries and run grocery stores here only because they cannot break the barriers of race and language.

Another stereotype: Asian Americans earn more on average than members of other ethnic groups. In fact, Mr. Takaki writes, family income surveys that draw such conclusions are misleading because Asian American families have more workers than other families, and because Asian Americans who earn the same amount as whites have done so mainly be acquiring more education. In the upper echelons of the working world, Asian Americans frequently encounter a "glass ceiling," he writes.

Growing up in Hawaii, Mr. Takaki had so many Asian American friends and neighbors that he never felt like a foreigner until he left the islands to attend the College of Wooster.

Mr. Takaki was an active participant in the debate at Berkeley over whether undergraduates should be required to take a course exploring the role of minority groups in the United States. He supported the proposal, which was adopted.

Mr. Takaki is the author of five earlier books, including Iron Cages: Race and Culture in 19th Century America. But unlike those more academic works, Strangers From a Different Shore was intended for a much broader audience.

In the judgment of a reviewer writing in *The New York Times Book Review*, Mr. Takaki succeeded. Declared the reviewer: "For the general reader, it is the best volume yet published on the subject."

In many ways, the book was a catharsis for Mr. Takaki, who interviewed his own relatives for it. He says the most satisfying part of his research was hearing – and later telling – stories that had not been told before. "I became a listener," he says. "Everywhere I went, Asian Americans were pouring their stories out to me."

Mr. Takaki recalls how, not long ago, he was taunted by a group of youngsters in California who asked why he did not "go back to China." He explained that he had never been to China, and that their comments hurt him, but he still wasn't sure his answer was effective.

He hopes that now he has offered a better answer.

4

Chapter

Three

Attacking the Problem of a Regional Image

Attacking the problem of regional image is one of the most important – and often most difficult – issues facing small and mid-size nonprofits, associations and corporations. It usually begins with trying to convince in-house staff and administration that there are sufficient reasons
for the implementation of a high-impact public relations program. Even
your own staff may ask, "Why do we want national publicity? We're not
a national institution."

Co-author Dick Jones, principal of Dick Jones Communications in
State College, Pa., explains that it may not be your intention to become a
national organization, but that national publicity lends a third-party
endorsement to your efforts. He says it's good to be a regional organization that's noticed nationally.

At Marywood University, the majority of the student body comes
from within a 100-mile radius. But that doesn't discourage the public
relations department from pitching stories to *The New York Times*, C-
SPAN or *Time Magazine*. When pitching a story, they make sure that
the issue is timely, trendy, or novel from a feature standpoint. If their
public relations staff pitches a comment from a professor on a timely
topic, they try to make sure that their source is very quotable.

The PR staff at Marywood thought they could capitalize on issues
pertaining to Catholic identity since the college was founded in 1915 as
one of the first Catholic Colleges for women in the United States. I
developed national media relations strategies based on its long history as
a Catholic institution of higher learning. Several op/eds on the topic were
placed on wire services and in major metropolitan papers. In addition, a

number of professors were quoted or had their research mentioned in a few national newspapers by way of trend stories. The alumni began to take notice, as did the rest of academia throughout the country. Marywood began to break free of its regional image.

The problems associated with a regional image do not confine themselves to members of the staff believing there is no merit in attempting to attract national exposure. Trying to convince members of the national press that your regional organization has something newsworthy to say is perhaps the most important element of any national media campaign.

Many national reporters do not suffer fools lightly. They need to be shown in quick fashion why a story is too important to be passed over. This means you have seven seconds to convey the essence of your story by phone. If they are reading your backgrounder, the first few sentences need to capture their interest. You must be succinct. If pitched properly, most reporters don't care where a good story comes from as long as it's of real news value or very innovative from a feature standpoint. Claremont McKenna College in California once received two separate full-page feature spreads in *The Washington Post* on research about William Shakespeare.

Professor Ward Elliott of Claremont McKenna College, a prestigious liberal arts college near Los Angeles, was bent on determining whether or not it would have been possible for William Shakespeare to have written all of the bodies of work attributed to the bard. A small but growing number of researchers were claiming that Edward de Vere, the 17th Earl of Oxford, actually composed the works. Professor Elliott set out to either prove or disprove this theory through computer-generated research that looked at such things as word frequency, punctuation proclivity, and the use of clauses and compounds. Professor Elliott reasoned that it should be possible to match that "signature" to the works of other claimants, including de Vere.

The reporter - in this case Don Oldenburg of *The Washington Post* - didn't care that the information came from Claremont McKenna, a small liberal arts college, and not Yale or Columbia.

Shakespeare by Any Other Name?
By Don Oldenburg
The Washington Post, April 17, 1990

On Saturday, in Claremont, Calif., the Claremont McKenna College professor will announce the official findings of the world's largest database of Elizabethan literature in search of evidence to support or dash claims that a 17th-century bumpkin from Stratford-on-Avon could not have written the Shakespeare cannon – therefore someone else did.

"It's like potato chips – one is not enough," says Elliott of the long list of claimants and pretenders to Shakespeare's throne. His voice rings eruditely Brahmin, so suitable for reciting the amassed verse he has examined via computers, virtually word by word, for the past three years while supervising The Shakespeare Clinic and its "matching Shakespeare" study.

Excerpt of an article from The Washington Post, © 1990. All rights reserved.

When we first suggested national publicity to Professor Elliott he seemed a little surprised. He had known that we were national media consultants, but to him that meant *The Los Angeles Times.* From his perspective, that's where he assumed we would try for a placement since Claremont is a short distance from Los Angeles. In this case, however, *The Los Angeles Times* would not have expanded the excellent regional image that Claremont McKenna had come to deserve. Instead, we decided to concentrate our efforts in the east in order to reach a market not normally available to Claremont McKenna. It was a bit risky at the time since the research was dated and we needed to place it as soon as possible. We were quite comfortable about our chances of scoring with *The Los Angeles Times*, but felt we needed to break out of a regional image. The methodology we used is explained throughout the remaining chapters.

Let's get back to an earlier point that reporters don't care where a story idea comes from, as long as it's a good idea. I vividly recall my first phone call to Mr. Oldenburg, a feature writer for *The Washington Post's* style section. I knew it was important to sell the Shakespeare story based on its merits, not its source. I reasoned that *The Washington Post* was looking to provide its readers with an array of newsworthy stories, no matter where they originated. Like all other papers, the *Post* had its own local news section where stories of regional interest were housed.

Knowing this was one thing. Trying to convince the Claremont professor whose research I was pitching was another matter all together. It seemed that Professor Elliott had his mind set on *The Los Angeles Times*. And although the placement certainly wasn't a sure thing, he believed that *The Los Angeles Times* would, by mere location, provide us with the best chance for exposure. My mind flashed back to an earlier conversation I had with Jack Stark, president of Claremont McKenna College. President Stark explicitly attained my services in order to expand Claremont College's image to a national audience.

Receiving support from the CEO or president to proceed with a national media relations plan is ultimately the first step for any institution. Reluctant presidents need to be convinced that national exposure is worth the time and investment involved. This can often be accomplished by stressing that national publicity benefits all components of an organization, both internally and externally. All constituencies of an organization are positively affected by a national placement. You can also mention to the president that national exposure tends to have a trickle down effect, and that once someone within the company receives national attention, others are likely to follow. Thus, it increases productivity at various levels.

I believed that the opportunity presented to me via professor Elliott's outstanding project was appropriate for a national audience. Mr. Oldenburg agreed within seconds of receiving my phone call. "It's exactly the type of story that I like to cover and that our readers like to read about," he said. Professor Elliott was extremely pleased.

National publicity doesn't always begin at the national level. Instead, it's sometimes necessary to begin with high-level regional publications such as *The Chicago Tribune*, *Dallas Morning News* or *Boston Globe*. Some of their circulation numbers are impressive.

Table B: Regional Daily Circulation Figures	
Publication	Circulation
Chicago Tribune	620,000
Long Island Newsday	573,000
Houston Chronicle	551,000
Dallas Morning News	489,000

San Francisco Chronicle	482,000
Boston Globe	473,000
Philadelphia Inquirer	430,000
Newark Star Ledger	402,000
Rocky Mountain News	392,000
Detroit Free Press	387,000
Denver Post	370,000
Miami Herald	357,000
The Oregonian	357,000
Baltimore Sun	327,000
Atlanta Journal-Constitution	327,000
New Orleans Times Picayune	270,000
Buffalo News	253,000
Pittsburgh Post Gazette	242,000
Louisville Courier-Journal	231,000
Seattle Times	230,000
Hartford Courant	216,000
Cincinnati Enquirer	195,000

(SOURCE: GEBBE PRESS "ALL IN ONE" DIRECTORY, COPYRIGHT 2000)

One good way of attacking a regional image is by parlaying successes with major regional newspapers into results with the national media. For instance, many national talk show assignment editors schedule guests through stories they read in the national papers. Tear sheets from an array of respected major metropolitan newspapers can produce similar results with talk show assignment editors.

Also, local newspaper stories can be carried nationally by wire services with which the paper is affiliated such as the Associated Press, Scripps Howard, Newhouse News Service, Knight Ridder News Service, Bridge News or Cox News Services. In addition, stories on local television stations can also be nationally syndicated through a national feed of the broadcast affiliation of the station.

Mercy Health Partners in Scranton, Pennsylvania became interested in national publicity and has used our services to that end. Mercy knows it does not have the far-reaching reputation of the Mayo Clinic. However, it has a sterling regional reputation as an outstanding heart hospital, among other areas of top specialties. Attaining national publicity would surely augment its fine regional image.

Unlike colleges that attract a portion of their student body from across the country, and thus use national publicity as an admissions tool, or companies that strive to increase sales nationally, the average regional health care system does not attract patients from across the country. Those seeking to break away from a regional image do so in order to increase their image with their local consumers. If *The New York Times* features a local hospital, then the people of that local community surely attach a greater significance to that hospital than they did previously. Also, that hospital can then highlight the fact that they received recognition from *The New York Times* in local ad campaigns and annual reports. In this case, breaking free from a regional image means enhancing your reputation with the constituents you seek to gain as consumers. You become a regional health care system that is recognized nationally, and surely that helps you become distinctive in your market.

One of the first things I did was a quick study on the important trade journals of the health industry. I discovered that *Modern Healthcare* magazine was considered the "Bible" of the health care industry. An article in *Modern Healthcare* is read by the major hitters of the health care industry and would bring a great deal of prestige to Mercy Health Partners. Although the editorial offices of *Modern Healthcare* are based in Chicago, the publication does have a bureau in New York City. I decided a visit to the bureau chief was in order.

An initial phone call to the editors at *Modern Healthcare* in New York went like this: "Hello, I represent Mercy Health Partners in Scranton. We have a project that includes pain management as the fifth vital sign, and thought you might be interested in hearing more about it. I'll be in New York within a few weeks and was wondering if you might have a few minutes to discuss pain management?"

At this initial contact, the public relations professional has only a few seconds to convey the merits of the particular program in very succinct, enthusiastic terms. Make crib notes about the program before the phone call so you do not hesitate if the reporter has questions for you.

"Well, Mercy has initiated a unique pain management program called 'Take the Fifth.' It's based on the theory that in addition to the four universally accepted vital signs, the level of pain a patient may be experiencing has now become the fifth vital sign. All Mercy nurses must take this fifth vital sign at least once during rounds."

"Sounds like a possible story," came the reply.

"If you have a few minutes on the 25th, I could stop by your office with some additional information for you. Besides, there are a few other programs at Mercy you might like to hear about."

With that, the media session was arranged. Once in New York at the office of *Modern Healthcare*, the conversation slowly moved from the topic of pain management to opinion editorials. I learned who the op/ed editor of *Modern Healthcare* was, and what type of essays she liked to receive. This information is very important since op/ed editors have different requirements and needs. Ironically, my focus for Mercy shifted almost immediately upon learning of a potential op/ed. I did leave the pain management information with the editor, but I understood that it might take several months to see that placement in the publication. A lot of things needed to fall in place for that to happen. On the other hand, an op/ed, if constructed properly, appeared to offer Mercy the best chances for a rather quick placement. Furthermore, an op/ed provides additional advantages that will be discussed in Chapter eight.

I learned from the New York editor that the op/ed editor of *Modern Healthcare* was based in Chicago and was interested in receiving pieces that cut across the full spectrum of health care, but the editor was particularly anxious to look at an op/ed that addressed the financial straits faced by hospitals. Armed with this important information, I spoke to Mercy's CEO, Mr. John Nespoli, and gathered background material on the subject, along with his personal thoughts and recommendations on ways to improve the situation.

Before I began the actual ghost writing process, (we find that most CEOs and presidents prefer to have the op/ed ghost written for them and then they are given final editing approval) I contacted the op/ed editor and pitched her our concept of an op/ed. She was very receptive and also surprised that someone would contact her to inquire about an op/ed's potential. "It's not often a person goes to that length to inquire about an op/ed," she said. Taking the time to make personal contacts is an invaluable tool of the trade. The more personal contacts you can nurture, the better the chance you have of succeeding with the national media.

After learning from the op/ed editor the specific op/ed requirements, such as style and length, I began the actual writing process. The final draft was presented to Mr. Nespoli for his changes. As is often the case, the CEO offered much insight and several sound editing changes. As the final version began to take form, Mr. Nespoli's opinion was clearly voiced.

The op/ed editor preferred that the piece be faxed to her. Other op/ed editors prefer e-mail. Within a few days, she called back with some minor suggestions which would improve the piece and make it more palatable for the readers' consumption. Since *Modern Healthcare* is a trade publication, the op/ed needed to be very specific and much more technical than, say, would an op/ed for a metropolitan newspaper with a more general audience. After two more edits by the op/ed editor and changes by Mr. Nespoli, the op/ed appeared in print.

The timing couldn't have been more perfect. The day it was published, Mr. Nespoli was scheduled to be at Mercy's corporate offices in Cincinnati. As he walked into the meeting, the CEO of Catholic Healthcare Partners (Mercy's corporate boss) passed copies of "What's a System To Do?" to everyone in attendance. He said being published in a prominent national publication made it a banner day for Mercy. They had broken free of their regional image in the minds of the thousands of healthcare executives across the country who read *Modern Healthcare.*

What's a system to do?
By John Nespoli
Modern Healthcare, September 20, 1999

We cannot give to the poor if we are one of them. Such has become the mantra for healthcare systems across the country that have perpetually given a sizable portion of their resources to provide for the poor and underserved.

The most recent date, from 1998, from the Pennsylvania Healthcare Cost Containment Council joint venture of government and business, included these statistics: 67% of hospitals cannot cover their operating costs with patient revenues; 54% of hospitals operate with net margins below what is sufficient to sustain financial viability over the long term; Balanced Budget Act of 1997 reductions in revenues over the next two years will remove more money from Medicare payments than all hospitals in the state now earn annually in net income; and Medicare and Medicaid account for 55% of hospital revenues. Pinpointing the main culprit behind the statistics is akin to deciding which Robert Frost stanza is the most harmonic.

In all likelihood, more than a third of the healthcare systems will face bankruptcies and consolidations in the coming years, which has enormous economic implications when health systems are the major employers in their communities.

The age of consumerism in healthcare has arrived. Consumers have access to once unobtainable health information through the Internet and other sources. They come to their physicians with options in hand. Patients will join payers in forcing providers to achieve radical improvements in all aspects of wellness, health management and healthcare delivery and financing. Those that don't meet the challenge will fail. Those that succeed will have a dramatic impact on the well-being and quality of the communities they serve.

*Reprinted with permission from **Modern Healthcare**.*
Copyright Crain Communications, Inc.
740 N. Rush Street, Chicago, IL 60611

In addition to enhancing a regional image, national publicity also strengthens the image of colleges, nonprofits and companies that are already recognized at the national level. There are many nationally recognized organizations that use national media relations plans to build upon their current name recognition.

Texas A&M University is a good example of an institution that felt the need to expand its fine national image to a level that would consistently provide the school with placements in *The New York Times, USA Today, Wall Street Journal,* and CNN. It appeared to us that the university had all the elements necessary to seriously pursue a national media relations plan – an energetic president, very active faculty with a strong research base, a financial commitment and skilled in-house public relations staff.

Located in College Station, 80 miles from Houston, Texas A&M is not exactly a hot bed of media activity. Texas A&M had long believed it played second fiddle to institutions like Penn State University. Although similar in many ways – both are large, land grant universities – the national media seemingly favored Penn State when seeking stories about higher education. This may or may not have been an accurate perception, but perception means an awful lot to those on the receiving end of publicity. Texas A&M was slighted, they thought, and ready to do something about it. The decree came from the top, President William Mobley. As Texas A&M's national media consultant, I was fortunate to have had direct access to Mr. Mobley on a number of occasions, a tactic that is imperative if a national campaign is to be successful.

Mr. Mobley surely knew the strengths and weaknesses of A&M and was confident that this nationally known university could begin to be recognized consistently by the national media over a period of time. He ultimately entrusted the strategy of national publicity to us and to top advisors within the school, with implicit instructions as to which directions he thought most appropriate to take.

Most notable were placements for the university's Military Studies Institute, whose faculty offered varied opinions during the Gulf War. These quotes appeared countless times throughout all major publications. In addition to the Military Studies Institute, I extensively used Dr. James McNeal, a faculty member whose expertise in the buying habits of children helped draw widespread attention to the university.

From the moment I first met Dr. McNeal, it was obvious that the affable professor of marketing understood the importance of having Texas A&M move to a consistent level of national recognition. He agreed to do what he could to help. His research on the buying power of children proved to be a very hot topic for the media. A number of clips in national publications on Professor McNeal's research assisted greatly in Texas A&M University's quest to become a national player in the eyes of the media. The methodology of landing these national placements, including the article excerpted below, will also be explained in detail throughout Chapters four through six.

The littlest consumers
By Lisa J. Moore
U.S. News & World Report, November 5, 1990

..."Newest and most earthshaking is the marketing to kids by companies that don't even sell children's products," says James McNeal, marketing professor at Texas A&M University and author

---

of Children as Consumers. Knowing that kids have a say in car buys these days, local car dealerships are running ads on WWTC-AM's "Radio Aahs," a new Minneapolis station featuring 24 hours of music, games, call-in quizzes and stories for kids under 12. Sports Illustrated for Kids boasts such heavy hitters as IBM and Centel. And over 200 firms from Apple to Polaroid now inundate schools with free teaching materials. However, informative as these are, the display of corporate logos can't help but garner name recognition.

Companies are courting the one market they feel is defying recession. According to surveys by Texas A&M's McNeal, some 37 million children from age 4 to 12 have nearly $9 billion of their own money and growing influence over Mom and Dad's cash. To grab a piece of that pie, a vast array of goods is emerging across a broad spectrum of quality.

Other nonprofits often face similar problems associated with a nationally known name but lack of national placements in the print and broadcast media. The Robert Wood Johnson Foundation of Princeton, New Jersey is an organization bursting with intellect, creativity and finances. It is by all measures one of the nation's premiere health care philanthropies. But according to officials at Robert Wood Johnson, it is also an organization that has not been brought in front of the general population through news articles and broadcast interviews as often as it would like to be.

"The only national publicity we get is through our PBS sponsorship of "All Things Considered"," a researcher at the foundation once remarked. Its overall image was certainly not something the Robert Wood Johnson Foundation needed to enhance. It had long enjoyed an excellent reputation among those within the health industry. However, the Robert Wood Johnson Foundation wanted to become a nationally recognized force in health issues. They turned to us for assistance.

We focused our attention on op/eds as a way of breaking free from a regional image and into the national spotlight. The results were almost immediate. A number of high profile placements were attained, including one in *The Washington Post*, which certainly boosted the national image of the Robert Wood Johnson. The methods used to develop and place these op/eds will be explained in full detail in Chapter eight.

> ## Rationing? It's Already Here
> By Steven A. Schroeder
> Excerpt from an article in the Washington Post, June 12, 1994
>
> . . .A question often heard in the debate about health care reform is whether it will be possible to achieve significant cost savings without rationing health care services. It is the wrong question. Health care rationing already occurs in the United States and in every other country as well.
> . . .The United States has difficulties in confronting health care rationing. We have deluded ourselves by rationing – for the most part – explicitly, while contending that rationing occurs in other countries, not in our own. As the escalating costs of medical care tear the veil that covers our rationing processes, we face the need for openly discussing difficult choices. It's time to start that conversation.
>
> *Reprinted from The Washington Post, © 1994. All rights reserved.*

Moving to a corporate example, the communications people at Compaq Computer in Houston wanted to increase the name recognition of their CEO and president, Eckhard Pfeiffer. Well known throughout the computer industry, Mr. Pfeiffer was widely credited with propelling Compaq to its number one status among makers of the personal computer. However, part of their corporate long-term strategy was to make Mr. Pfeiffer a recognizable commodity throughout all sectors of the business world. Moreover, the people at Compaq wanted Mr. Pfeiffer to be known within the entertainment industry since the "Grand Alliance" – a group of Hollywood executives and computer makers – was pushing the Federal Communications Commission for the use of interlace transmission feed for digital TV.

Suave and learned, Mr. Pfeiffer is a PR consultant's dream. But in order to market him effectively, we had to develop a very detailed national media plan. To enhance Mr. Pfeiffer's previous national media placements, we decided to concentrate our initial efforts on *USA Today,*

The New York Times and *The Christian Science Monitor.* We believed that this combination would get Mr. Pfeiffer more mainstream press, and through *The New York Times* and *USA Today,* into the homes of millions of readers. As for *The Christian Science Monitor,* its nationally syndicated op/ed page would be the perfect way to have Mr. Pfeiffer air his personal views without fear of editing or being misquoted.

This is a prime example of a powerful corporation desiring to have its CEO break from the ranks of trade publications and periodic national press and lunge into the mainstream of the national media. It was not enough that Mr. Pfeiffer was widely known and respected throughout the computer industry. Moving to the highest level of name recognition would accomplish several goals for Compaq Computer Corporation. The PR people at Compaq had already done a wonderful job getting Mr. Pfeiffer into national publications. Their telecommunications consultant decided that with our assistance, such media coverage could be achieved on a more consistent basis.

After successful placements in *The New York Times, USA Today* and *The Christian Science Monitor,* it was time for an interview with *Variety,* the trade journal of Hollywood. After all, Mr. Pfeiffer needed to be viewed as a "player" by the tinsel town crowd since computers would certainly be impacting the entertainment industry in the near future. We also knew that a *Variety* placement, combined with the other placements, would surely help Mr. Pfeiffer distance himself from a perceived regional image within the computer industry.

Enhancing a national reputation or breaking free from a regional image means different things for different clients. For colleges and universities, even those that don't or never will attract a large percentage of students from outside a small radius, being recognized nationally will enhance their regional reputation by receiving strong third-party endorsements. Public relations directors at colleges and universities always feel good about their work when they receive that special feature in their local newspaper. Imagine the feeling they get when *The New York Times* features one of their professors or students. And those same public relations directors can parlay national publicity into even bigger results by including the clips in creative ad campaigns and annual reports.

Corporations can use national publicity as a means of bolstering stockholder confidence in a company that has been recognized at the national level. A consistent national media relations campaign can assist the CEO in his or her efforts of becoming recognized among colleagues as a major player within a particular industry, and in some instances can help to increase productivity, sales, or market share.

Chapter

Four

Identifying Stories for National Publicity

Identifying stories is the first element for any national media plan. Which story ideas will sell? Which will capture the attention of a national reporter? Most stories that concern employee appointments, promotions or routine in-house activities are low impact and will certainly not be of interest to any national reporter. There are a number of stories that tend to attract national attention more readily than others. Look for interesting campus or corporate traditions as a way to break into the national spotlight.

At Marywood University, an annual tradition of having the president of the university serve lunch to students to encourage service activities resulted in a photo and feature in the Education Life supplement of *The New York Times*. I pitched the fact that Marywood University's mission included a kind of moral compass through various courses that help shape a student's character. The school created a theme, "Living Responsibly in an Interdependent World," and incorporated it into the curriculum to set a standard against which all academic endeavors are evaluated.

"Whether you're on a secular campus or a religious campus, I think that question is being raised all over the country," responded Sister Mary Reap, President of Marywood University, when asked whether colleges ought to try to build moral and spiritual character as well as intellect.

As a result, Marywood University created a new position called Coordinator of Mission Enhancement, whose job description included assisting students in their search for God, truth and the Gospel. I identified these elements as having national news potential. They were part of a national movement that was quickly gaining recognition. And although many other schools across the country were participating in similar activities, the fact that Marywood University included it as part of their curriculum surely increased its news value. Also, we were the first one to bring the issue to the education reporters at *The New York Times*. This always helps. In the end, Marywood was featured in the following excerpt that also included the University of Notre Dame.

Colleges Setting Moral Compasses
New York Times, August 4, 1996

. . .But now, in a time of outward tension and inner searching, when many Americans worry about social decay and also show a growing interest in spirituality, students, teachers and administrators on campus are asking whether colleges ought to try once again to build moral and spiritual character as well as intellect.

"Whether you're on a secular campus or a religious campus, I think that question is being raised all over the country," said Sister Mary Reap, president of Marywood College, a Roman Catholic institution in Scranton, Pa. "Any meeting of university presidents I've been in, we're concerned about the lack of ethical standards of some who've been through our schools."

. . .Sister Mary said that volunteer work is highly popular among the current generation of college students, so Marywood has no problem finding applicants for the programs. But she added that while she encourages

Reprinted from The New York Times, © 1996. All rights reserved.

Another example of a tradition that received national publicity comes from one small college in central Pennsylvania that offers scholarships to left-handers. And although the actual worth is limited in value, the yearly tradition never fails to find a place at the national level.

Without sound news judgment, even the most creative national media campaign will fall flat on its face. A good story, not the strategy itself, must always be the focal point for any national media plan. This is precisely why many corporations and nonprofits hire former news reporters to head their public relations staffs. Someone who once sat behind a newsroom's news desk is often more likely to recognize the merits of a news story than is a person trained strictly in public relations.

One national education editor was known for his propensity to throw letters from a particular university (its letterhead was on the return address) into the trash without even bothering to open the envelopes to see what possible story idea may have lurked inside. When asked by a colleague why he did this, the editor responded: "If their PR office can't decide which stories have national news potential, I won't do it for them." It seems this particular university had a habit of inundating national education editors with every press release ever written by their PR staff, without regard to its national news value. After a few weeks, the frustrated education editor simply stopped opening letters from the university. Needless to say, this university never saw one of its stories placed at the national level.

The ability to say "no" is extremely important for any national media consultant. More often than not, the stories you encounter within the confines of a college, nonprofit or corporation are not conducive to national exposure. You'll be asked by faculty, researchers and CEOs to get them into *The New York Times*, but the story ideas they sometimes offer can be benign or lifeless. Once, while consulting for a large research university, I was told that an exciting feature possibility was lurking in the science department. I was escorted to the laboratory by the head of the public relations department and came upon a scientist who had devoted his entire adult life's work to studying the migratory habits of the red ant. My ensuing interview with the bespectacled gentleman rendered little or no information that, in my opinion, warranted national publicity.

True, he had studied the wandering habits of the little creatures for years upon year and could predict the precise patterns of the movement of red ants. But the information was not earth shattering or even novel from a feature standpoint. The national media would not be interested. This was an opinion the professor did not want to hear and he proceeded to talk more and more about the intricacies of his research. Still not for the layman, I contended. Perhaps for a trade journal, but not *Newsweek*.

You need to trust your news judgment and stand by your convictions. After all, you are the expert in the area of media relations, not the CEO or professor. Trust your gut instincts. In time, identifying stories that have national news potential becomes second nature. And you'll be pleasantly surprised how much respect you'll receive from your clients by being firm about your conclusions. It's far better to state your opinion that a story doesn't have national news potential at the onset than promising it will appear in *National Geographic* when you know that result is unlikely. Misleading someone will only hurt your credibility. And as a consultant or public relations professional, your credibility is everything.

One of the best ways to get a feel for what the national media are looking for is to scan the national publications each day and notice articles that are similar to those you may be pitching. Of course, you would never want to pitch a story idea to a reporter who has already covered that exact subject. Just look for similar articles and reporters who cover similar topics.

Identifying stories is not an exact science, and your judgment may sometimes be incorrect. During my first campus visit to the University of California Berkeley, an admissions counselor mentioned that the students had planned numerous events to celebrate the first Earth Day. She wondered if there might be national publicity potential here. I informed her that Earth Day would probably not receive national coverage since it was one of many "days" that are finding their way onto calendars. You can imagine my surprise when *The New York Times* featured several colleges and universities throughout the country and their Earth Day activities. The crow didn't taste too good, but I admitted my error in judgment and proceeded to look at other possible news stories.

One of these stories came from Ron Takaki, the professor of Asian-American studies whose book, *Strangers From a Different Shore: A History of Asian Americans*, received quite a bit of national attention once we established a national media plan for the soft spoken professor.

How did we ascertain that Professor Takaki's book would stand out among the hundreds of books published each year by those in higher education? How did we identify his as potentially newsworthy for the national media? Attaining national publicity for Mr. Takaki began with the mere fact that his book was very good and timely. It came at a time when a lot of attention was being focused on whether or not higher education was devoting enough attention to the issue of diversity. Thus *Stranger From a Different Shore* became part of a larger trend story.

In addition to what we considered to be a good trend story was Professor Takaki's infectious enthusiasm about his work. As consultants we quickly embraced his love of the topic. This is no small point to be made here. Without an enthusiastic and quotable source, your chances of attaining national publicity are almost non-existent.

When we discovered that students at Marywood University were involved with a national arts projects called "Save Outdoor Sculpture" that included refurbishing worn sculptures on campus that had become decimated through the effects of weathering and, in some cases, vandalism, it became apparent that this project might be newsworthy to the national media. First and foremost, it was part of a national effort that claimed to be the largest cultural volunteer project in the U.S. As many as 15,000 people in all 50 states had committed to the project. Being part of such a first-time national effort made this a relatively easy story to identify as a possible feature for the national media.

When identifying stories, it is important to look at the background and experience of the person who will be the source of the publicity. Has the CEO or professor written any previous books? Professor Takaki had authored five earlier books, a fact not lost on national reporters who are looking for credible sources. Add the fact that Mr. Takaki was an active participant in the debate at Berkeley over whether undergraduates should be required to take a course exploring the role of minority groups in the United States, and you have the makings of a nice trend story.

A trend story looks at society and issues that affect a large number of people. These are popular with the media because readers are anxious to know about the latest trends or fads. National trends are excellent vehicles. Where does your organization fit in? Take, for instance, the National Disability Act – not exactly an everyday, newsworthy item. But as its fifth anniversary approached, one small eastern college gathered its resources and looked at what it has been doing to comply with the law. A few weeks in advance, tip sheets, including quotes, were faxed to a well-conceived list of national reporters who would likely be looking at the issue. The results were two national mentions for the school's professors and a feature on one of its students in *USA Today*.

Earth Day quickly became entrenched in the national mindset as a notable occurrence, and thus became a trend story each year for the national media. National health days that raise the level of awareness for a plethora of diseases are often covered in one format or another by the national media. Those industrious public relations directors or consultants who seek national publicity will gather human interest material weeks before each "health day" in order to call a list of selected health reporters. You can get calendars and books that list each "national" day or month for particular topics such as health or education. Beware of going overboard with this approach to trend stories. It is prudent to concentrate on those days you have seen covered in the past as opposed to trying to find story ideas for each one.

Features can also be garnered through personality profiles. Pitching the quirks or interesting characteristics of a CEO, nonprofit director, college president or expert staffer can surely work to your advantage. Take Eckhard Pfeiffer, for example. This former CEO of Compaq Computer had attained a well-earned reputation as a top corporate manager. Furthermore, his background is quite interesting. A German by birth, Pfeiffer led Compaq to its lofty status as the number one PC maker in the world within a four-year span, well ahead of even his own predictions. Known as a man who loves to have fun, Pfeiffer has been featured in such publications as *Fortune* for not only his business acumen but also for his love of the dance floor.

The personality feature, however, is not without risks. The public may view personality quirks as strange and undesirable – a phenomenon known as the Howard Hughes syndrome. If, for example, a CEO like Pfeiffer likes to drive fast and dance the night away at Houston nightclubs, that fact alone surely won't merit national attention. Couple this with a very strong performance by Compaq, and his personal passion becomes a sign of a strong leader who exhibits a humanistic side. It's the context of the feature that counts the most.

The personality feature won't (and shouldn't) stand alone. It must be combined as a pitch to the national media with newsworthy information in order to have a chance. In Pfeiffer's case, the pitch was the remarkable performance of Compaq after Pfeiffer took over the reins, combined with his outgoing personality.

The research of a University of Iowa professor helped him become a nationally known advocate for people with disabilities, and also resulted in some high profile personality placements. Professor Peter Blanck has collected an impressive array of data on the Americans With Disabilities Act over the years. This in itself has led to many national clips, especially as a trend story during the anniversary of the Disabilities Act. However, it was his work with a baseball card company that attracted some human-interest features. Professor Blanck offered his services to help create baseball cards that featured former professional baseball players who had some form of disability. The results were a number of human-interest features throughout the national print and broadcast media, such as this New York Times excerpt:

Data on Disabilities True and False
By Barbara Presley Noble
New York Times, July 19, 1992

Among the early pages of a new study on the impact of the Americans With Disabilities Act is a chart listing 10 dearly held attitudes about people with disabilities and their ability to work.

. . .Perhaps the study's author, Peter David Blanck, a law professor at the University of Iowa and a fellow of the Annenberg Foundation, a nonpartisan research group based in Washington, could have simply incorporated the 10 into his text, but that would have lessened the impact of what appears just to the right of each statement: The word "False," forming a 10-rung ladder of reproach down the column.

The human-interest feature is a very effective way to attract national attention for your institution. All companies and non-profits have interesting traditions or quirky projects that may raise the eyebrows of a national reporter. And these may result in mentions or small placements. In all likelihood, it may be the human-interest feature article that draws the most attention because the human-interest article normally carries with it the most words and often a photo that accompanies the story.

To identify potential feature articles, you must look beyond the traditions and trends and into the substantive research and accomplishments of the company or college, or persona of the CEO or president. The first time I met Bill Glavin, president of Babson College, his presence and command of a room immediately attracted my attention. Here was a man of importance, and surely someone with an interesting story to tell. His six-foot, seven-inch frame was imposing enough, and his keen intellect was evident after hearing him speak for just a few minutes. But it was his background that I believed would help draw him, and thus Babson, the national attention it was seeking. A former vice chairman of the Xerox corporation, Mr. Glavin's 34 years of business experience made him the ideal candidate to head the small business college that was looking for a strong president to enhance its image. Mr. Glavin was also at a point in his life where retirement sounded appealing to someone who loved to golf. I believed that a reporter for a national paper or national trade publication might be interested in the reason behind Bill Glavin coming to Babson.

Herein lies another way of identifying potential national news stories. If the subject interests you and arouses an unbridled curiosity in you, why wouldn't it do the same to a reporter? Trust your natural instincts.

Other elements to look for in trying to identify possible national feature stories are the special appeal they may have to a selected group of readers and the "first-time-ever-told" litmus test. Horse racing is a major industry across the United States that appeals to hundreds of thousands of people who either go to the tracks, place wagers at off-track betting sites, or watch racing events such as the running for the roses.

This special appeal and first-time-ever-told litmus test became the basis for a feature placement in *The New York Times* for the University of Louisville. Professor Robert Lawrence headed, of all things, the university's racetrack management program. And although this wasn't the only such program in the country, we were not aware of any published story about racetrack management at a college. Professor Lawrence and I managed to convince Elizabeth Fowler, the careers columnist at *The New York Times*, that this story would carry a special appeal to all the people who enjoy horse racing throughout the country.

Learning To Manage A Race Track
Elizabeth M. Fowler
Article excerpt from The New York Times, May 1, 1990

"The racing world will be here this week, and we will be busy taping interviews to be used in class," Dr. Robert Lawrence, a professor at the University of Louisville, said the other day. He heads its race track management program. Then on Saturday he and many students are off to the races – the Kentucky Derby at nearby Churchill Downs.

. . .Being a horse lover is not enough to qualify a student for the program, Dr. Lawrence said, explaining that the industry needs better trained personnel in accounting, financial management, computer science and public relations.

Plugging organizational expertise into breaking news or seasonal stories can be productive, but the strategy requires quick action. One midwestern university has a professor within its ranks who has conducted research of airplane disasters and can easily recite various statistics concerning safety records. Whenever a mishap or near crash occurs, the professor's name and background is immediately faxed or e-mailed to a preconceived list of appropriate reporters.

The success rate for any national pitch, including trend or human interest stories, is small. Depending on the size of your staff, only a certain amount of time can be devoted to trend stories each month. Compiling an accurate mailing or fax list – a must – can take away precious time from the nuts and bolts operation of a small PR staff. As Dick Jones, whose firm works within the higher education field, explains, "It's usually wrong to fault the public relations office for a lack of high-impact programs. Most campus PR shops are staffed with extremely qualified people." The problem, he contends, is not a dearth of talent, energy or good ideas. The problem is too few staff members and too little time.

Without the help of a consultant, small public relations shops must make prudent decisions about when and how to attain a degree of national exposure. A misguided plan will only result in frustration. We suggest our clients use work-study students or interns to help with national publicity efforts, including having them compile updated media lists. Also, have these students type personal envelopes to each reporter, rather than relying on labels. Most word processing programs can also do this job. There's a slightly better chance that a reporter will open a letter with a hand-typed address as opposed to a label. Any edge you can give yourself helps. Actually, sending unsolicited news releases is not a very effective way to attain national publicity, but every now and then it does work. Don't neglect it totally.

In addition to campus traditions and national trends, most campuses have newsworthy scholarship to tout. All colleges have professors who routinely conduct research or surveys, and it's your job to decipher the newsworthy stuff from the rest of the academic jargon. It was research on the Americans With Disabilities Act that got Professor Blanck into *The New York Times* as part of a feature article. Professor Blanck's enthusiasm helped convince us that his research had national news written all over it. His enthusiasm also helped convince the reporter. Add the fact that Professor Blanck was very witty, and you had the makings of a good feature story. It was his impressive, exhaustive research that landed Professor Blanck on the pages of *The New York Times,* along with several other prominent placements. The operative word here is research. With few exceptions, unique or interesting research can do more for your organization than anything else in terms of national recognition.

The key to turning research papers into news stories is making them accessible to the average reader. This does not mean "dumbing down" the research. It does mean turning academic and professional jargon into understandable English. Any person with a logical mind should be able to examine a research paper, extract the key points and tell enough about the methodology and impact of the work to interest journalists.

Research that impacts all of us stands the most chance of being picked up. When a researcher at Hope College in Holland, Michigan received a grant to study the impact of forgiveness on the physical well being of people, Dick Jones thought he had a good story. Everyone, after all, is in a position to forgive and be forgiven, usually several times a day. *Time Magazine* and CNN thought it was a good story too. And it didn't matter that it came from Hope College and not the University of Michigan. A good story is a good story.

Should All Be Forgiven?
By David Van Biema
Article excerpt from Time Magazine, April 5, 1999

Step into a forgiveness laboratory partly funded by a $75,000 Templeton grant. At Hope College in Holland, Mich., Charlotte van Oyen Witvliet puts electrodes on a young volunteer. In a moment, he will think about a hurt that has been done him and then "actively rehearse" it for 16 seconds. At the sound of a tone, he will escalate his thoughts to "nursing a grudge" and making the offender feel horrible. Another beep will cue him to shift gears and "empathize with the offender." Finally, he will imagine ways to "wish that person well." Throughout the two-hour session, the four responses occur in different sequences, and Witvliet, a professor of psychology, will measure his heart rate, blood pressure, sweat and muscle tension.

. . .But interviews with her subjects indicate that they felt in even greater control when they tried to empathize with their offenders and enjoyed the greatest sense of power, well-being and resolution when they managed to grant forgiveness. "If you are willing to exert the effort it takes to be forgiving, there are benefits both emotionally and physically," she concludes.

Even if you work for an organization without a research component, don't forget that you can commission polls, surveys and studies that will advance the interests of your firm while providing opportunities for media coverage. National reporters, especially those who work for the wire services, love polls or surveys and will often consider academic papers that include surveys for a national wire story. As a public relations pro, it's your responsibility to decide which surveys will appeal to a lay audience.

Chapter
Five

Story Development/Story Marketing

After you've identified potential national news stories, it's time to develop them into a package that could result in major media visibility. Story development and marketing begins by deciding if a story can stand on its own merits or needs to be combined into a trend or roundup story. Despite pleas from CEOs and nonprofit presidents, it's not possible to pitch every story as an exclusive feature for one particular institution or company.

Trend stories present frequent options, but they can also detract greatly from other tasks of a small public relations office. If you happen to be the University of Michigan or Coca Cola, you perhaps have the luxury of a staff person devoted solely to national media relations. The University of California Berkeley at one point provided office space for the far western *New York Times* stringer. Most PR offices are not so fortunate. Therefore, deciding on which stories to pitch is a major part of any high-impact campaign for small and medium public relations shops.

Roundup Stories

During the Gulf War, a number of small colleges successfully used the "roundup" story method to break into the national spotlight. Armed with quotes from various faculty, these colleges knew from scanning the newspapers which reporters were specifically covering the war. Some quick phone calls, followed by faxes with quotes from professors, resulted in numerous mentions for small colleges.

National reporters like to hear from public relations people who are armed with a good roundup story. It gives the story a lot more credibility if it happens to include information about more than one company or institution. For example, each year the SAT scores are national news.

Whether or not the test scores are rising is of concern to a large portion of the population. Headlines announcing the latest results are attention grabbers.

Let's assume, for example, that "Old Siwash" University wanted to promote its enviable SAT scores and the fact that they had increased by 20 percent over the past decade, all this while increasing their minority admissions. Going to *The Washington Post* with only their test results would in all likelihood result in an exercise in futility. "Too much propaganda," a *Post* reporter would surely surmise. If, on the other hand, Siwash took the initiative and managed to include test results from other schools across the country, both large and small, they would stand a much better chance of having their scores published.

There are other forms of roundup stories that don't necessarily relate to annual events such as the SATs, or breaking news like the Gulf War. Roundup stories can be created on an ad hoc basis, depending on the situation. For example, staffers at Dick Jones Communications learned that many of the schools it served had food service programs where students could bring recipes from home and the dining hall would prepare them. This was perfect for a roundup story and resulted in a front-page placement in *The Wall Street Journal* for several of the institutions.

Another example of a good roundup story centers on financial milestones or annual events, such as tax time. You can be sure that each year, all of the national publications will publish articles on the trendiest tax issues, be it on-line filing or the latest in creative deductions. If your company happens to be an accounting or consulting firm, or if you work for a university whose business school wants to gain some national attention, dig deep for interesting ways you can file returns. You might even identify a person who has a unique story to tell about the IRS and who is willing to talk with the national media.

Feature Stories

Perhaps you're the PR director for a Wall Street brokerage firm and you'd like to have your CEO included on the news broadcasts as one of the many talking heads they use each time the market fluctuates. To have your CEO stand apart from the rest, maybe he or she would be willing to make some bold predictions about the future of the market. Many CEOs shy away from this approach, but it can be done. Perhaps your company has established a niche for itself in one particular area, such as electronics, and a major merger just took place. Let the national media know that your CEO can address the issue and is very good with sound bites.

Feature stories, as opposed to roundups or trends, are obviously the preferable choice for any institution and require much time, patience and resolve. There are several strategies that can increase your odds of landing that coveted feature story in a national publication. Begin by trusting your own news judgment, especially if you happen to come from a newspaper background. If not, it's a good idea to hire someone who has newspaper experience. In fact, most companies and colleges are now doing precisely this. Someone who sat on the receiving end of pitch letters and phone calls is far more likely to understand the intricacies of the business than someone who comes strictly from the public relations side.

There is really no substitute for good news judgment. It's an invaluable asset for anyone in the public relations profession. Sadly enough, good news judgment is normally not taught in public relations classes at today's colleges and universities. Little by little this skill is being eroded from the minds of those aspiring to be part of the news business. Much of what is ingrained into the minds of public relations students today appears to emphasize hype. They assume that the louder the message, then the better the chance of reaching an audience.

More often than not, having good news judgment begins with having personal writing experience. This may come in many forms. It's quite acceptable if you got your start in the business by writing for a small weekly newspaper. Or perhaps you free lanced for a community magazine. Maybe your first writing experience came in high school for the school newspaper, followed by a stint at the college newspaper.

Writing begets good writing. Eventually, good writing becomes habitual. We're not talking the Pulitzer Prize here, but we've seen far too many aspiring public relations students who can't match a subject and predicate. Just as good writing becomes second nature, so does the art of good news judgment. The more you read feature articles in the respected papers, the more you'll get a feel for what constitutes a good story. Not all story ideas presented to you by your clients or place of employment will be suitable for framing. Pitching a story to a lifestyle editor about a professor who studies the migratory habits of the red ant won't get you a permanent place in that reporter's Rolodex.

The concept of developing a feature story must be well crafted and molded in many directions along the way. A feature we developed for the Marian Miner Cook Athenaeum at Claremont McKenna College in California comes to mind. I'll never forget walking into the Athenaeum one spring evening. I had just completed my first campus visit to the college and was looking forward to relaxing at a wine and cheese party for some faculty and upper classmen. All I knew about the pending evening was that the president of the college and his wife would be hosting the informal affair, and that there would be a speaker talking to both faculty and students about an issue of the day.

When identifying and developing stories, it is imperative that you, as the consultant or public relations director, talk directly – face to face if possible – with the researcher or CEO (the object of the possible story). This is why we visit campuses or corporate headquarters several times each year. It's hard to get a feel for a national news story without hearing it told to you directly from the source.

The Athenaeum building occupies the center of Claremont's pristine campus. Several times each week students and faculty attend events at the Athenaeum, which can include talks by the famous – the Reverend Jesse Jackson among them – or informal discussions between mentors and students. There were no well-known speakers the day I was there, but the intimate, scholarly atmosphere of the Athenaeum immediately struck me as a place where learning beyond the classroom walls could occur for Claremont's 800 undergraduates.

Although I had been introduced to several prominent professors who showed me all kinds of research during my campus visit, I wondered if I hadn't walked into a setting that presented the best possibility for national publicity. It contained the necessary elements: a special appeal to a wide, general audience, and a "first time ever told" aspect. The Athenaeum appeared to be able to stand on its own as a story, and it did not need to be combined into a trend story.

My initial thoughts were to develop this for *The New York Times* Education Supplement, a quarterly publication that looks at all levels of education and attracts a very large audience. And although many of us in the public relations business at the time had begun to feel that the *Times* was devoting more and more space to elementary and high schools at the expense of higher education, I nonetheless decided that the Athenaeum would be a nice fit for the Education Supplement. As it turned out, the education editor for *The New York Times* decided that the story wasn't right for them.

This was not the first time that a story idea of mine had been turned down by a national reporter. Because of factors beyond your control, such as limited space in newspapers and reporters' own agendas, having a national reporter bite on one of your pitches is indeed the exception and not the rule. But because of all the benefits associated with a national placement, even a small percentage of placements are worth all the effort you've expended.

I had established a very good rapport with an education reporter for *The Christian Science Monitor*, and although it is not as widely circulated as other national newspapers, the paper does reach many of the major cities in the country. Its reporting is consistently considered first rate and it became clear to me that the Monitor would be my second choice.

Living Room Lures Collegians
By Laurel Shaper Walters
Christian Science Monitor, November 26, 1990

"I am a certified 'Athaholic'," confesses John McIntire, a senior here at Claremont McKenna College, 35 miles east of Los Angeles near the San Gabriel mountains. Micah Jacobson, a freshman at the college, makes the same admission in a different way. "I'm an Athenaeum junkie," he says.

These college students are not talking about substance abuse. Far from it. John and Micah are attracted to the "intellectual smorgasbord" of the college's Marian Miner Cook Athenaeum. . . .

Several times a week, John and Micah, along with hundreds of other students and faculty here, attend events at the Athenaeum. It serves as a meeting house and alternative dining hall for students, faculty, and a roster of visitors.

Feature story ideas come in many forms. Research-oriented features are probably the most effective, and Texas A&M University surely used their industrious faculty to their advantage in the early part of the 1990s. Dr. James McNeal, the consumer buying professor, was featured in no less than five national publications and appeared on two national talk shows. Surely Texas A&M is a large university, but smaller colleges and corporations can reap the same results if they can locate their "shining star" on campus or in the research department and routinely pitch his or her research or area of expertise to all national outlets.

Strategies for Making Contact

We strongly suggest that you phone national reporters to inform them of a story idea, or to let them know that background material will be coming in the mail. There's really no substitute for this approach. Also, do your homework and make sure you know which reporter is covering which area. There's nothing more embarrassing than reaching a reporter and being told, "I haven't covered that beat in two years." Don't rely on outdated media guides. Scan the national papers routinely and keep abreast of the various assignments. Phone calls and updated media guides are necessary to learning the assignments of editors at major television and radio broadcast outlets. For this reason, Dick Jones Communications does not allow its staffers to depend on pre-prepared media lists. "We want our people to work to make sure that every individual who receives a pitch letter is the current person covering the beat," says Jones.

Remember that your phone calls must be concise. Reporters can be curt and quite uninterested in hearing from someone in public relations. On the other hand, we do find that some reporters welcome ideas for a good news story and will be receptive. It may surprise you to learn that many national reporters never receive such pitch calls because most people in the public relations profession don't use this personal approach. They are either too intimidated by the national media, or they believe that sending out hundreds of nameless, unsolicited news releases will work for them.

We've talked to public relations directors who have said, "You just can't pick up the phone and call someone at *Newsweek*." When we tell them that it is possible to do just that and then meet with reporters in New York or Washington, D.C. for media sessions, the public relations directors act astounded. I once remarked to John Stossel of ABC's "20/20" that he must be inundated with calls from public relations people across the country. His answer was a resounding "no." "Hardly ever," he said. "I guess people are too intimidated by the national media to pick up the phone and call someone like me."

Working with Reporters

When we consulted for the Amazing Maize Maze, one of the first human-sized mazes cut through a cornfield, we did not need to identify the story. It was already there for us in Lancaster County, Pennsylvania next to the Strasburg Rail Road. Its founder, Don Frantz, a co-producer of Disney's Broadway spectacular "Beauty and the Beast," understood the concepts of promotion quite well. He knew he had a unique product, and one that could be developed into several national media stories. In addition to the elements of a good feature story, it obviously has one more thing going for it – the visual aspect. The Amazing Maize Maze did have one minor drawback. Because the maize was a perishable product, the time frame for attaining a national feature was quite constricted. A news conference seemed out of the question. There was really no "news" per se to announce. Also, the timing of the corn at its ripest stage, imperative for photos, would be too tricky to predict far enough ahead of time to allow for reporters to get it on their schedules.

We decided on a strategy that would combine the elements of a news conference with the personal touch of a media session. Instead of going to the reporter, as in the case of most media sessions, we would ask the reporters to come to us for a tour, one at a time or as a group. This will be explained more fully in Chapter six, Target Marketing. The point here is that we developed and packaged the story as a feature to stand on its own merits. It did not need to be combined as a trend story or one that focused on research.

You can receive national attention without confining yourself to research. Look for strong departmental stories that happen to correlate to the news of the day. If you work for a college, don't limit yourself to education reporters simply because the story has originated from a college campus. Locate feature writers, business reporters, sports writers, and lifestyle editors. If your art department has a story to tell, try contacting the art reporter at national media outlets. Look for columnists who write weekly columns on specific topics. For instance, Gehrung Associates practically made a living dealing with three columnists during the late 1980s: a career columnist and a parent/child columnist, both from *The New York Times,* and a management columnist for *Fortune Magazine.*

The *Fortune* columnist, like many other national reporters and columnists, welcomed media sessions with sources he believed could

offer insights for his column. We had developed a very good professional relationship with the columnist over the years, and he respected our
ability to offer him some of the finest minds in the field of business.

Rather than developing a story idea for him that would be the focus
of his entire column, we knew from experience that he liked to use a
number of sources within each column. This was quite different from
the career columnist for *The New York Times*, who would often base
her entire column on one program or person.

There were basically two ways we would develop a story idea for the
Fortune columnist. The first resulted from periodic phone calls we
would place to the columnist in order to inquire if there were any particular ideas for future columns that he'd be willing to share with us. If that
were the case, we would offer our assistance by providing some quotable
professors or corporate executives.

On other occasions we would call with a preconceived story idea
that emanated from our meetings with various clients. We would suggest
to our client, "I think what you've just said may be of interest to a columnist with *Fortune Magazine*. Are you willing to talk with him on the
phone, or better yet meet with him in New York City?"

Once we had developed an initial story line, we then needed to
gather other sources that also looked at the same topic but perhaps from
another perspective. Armed with a variety of viewpoints on the topic,
along with some pithy quotes, we would call the columnist and either
offer to fax him the information or request a meeting at his office with
one or two of the sources. The following excerpt shows the kinds of articles that can result.

Overscheduled And Not Loving It
By Walter Kiechel III
Fortune Magazine, April 8, 1991

The tendency to take on too much can also spill over into the mea-
ger remnants of your personal life. If you take on something new,
give up something you were doing. It may help to ask yourself the
following questions with some frequency:

Should I, in all my loftiness, be doing this? Michael Abelson, a management professor at Texas A&M University, argues that there are

only six things an executive should never delegate: planning, selecting the team, monitoring their effort (not "How ya doing?" but "Where are you in the project?"), motivating, evaluating, and rewarding them.

Speeches

Other ways of identifying stories stem from texts of speeches that may be excerpted for use in roundup stories. For example, most national news outlets carry some form of coverage during commencement time. Well-known speakers can obviously attract some attention, as can less-known celebrities if their topic is timely. Controversy in a speech doesn't hurt. Once again, timing is everything and PR offices need to get an advance copy of the speech in order to determine its news value.

Editorial Board Meetings

Editorial board meetings can be a very important aspect of a well-defined national media relations plan. An editorial board meeting consists of gathering together a newspaper's editors (those who work on the editorial page along with the op/ed editor) and also selected reporters who cover a particular beat. For example, if the topic of the editorial board is computers, the reporter for that beat should be at the editorial board meeting. Like any other aspect of media relations, being granted an editorial board meeting by a newspaper takes planning and initiative on the part of the public relations office or media consultant.

The purpose is to present a particular viewpoint to the newspaper with the hope that the publication will endorse the stance of the company or institution. The specific request for endorsement must be made clear during the meeting. For example, the Annenberg Washington program wanted to highlight the need for better communications concerning the need for increased organ donations among the general population. As the program's national media relations consultants, we thought that arranging an editorial board meeting would present the best opportunity to air the program's concerns about organ transplants. After all, no news story was attached to this particular problem. And although the

Annenberg Washington Program had conducted extensive research into the situation, it wasn't the type of material that lent itself to a news release or standard media session with a singular reporter.

Armed with a wealth of background information on the topic, we contacted the editorial department of *The Wall Street Journal* and outlined the need for a stepped-up effort to raise the public's awareness of the need for a higher percentage of organ donors. We explained our position in succinct terms backed by our research, and requested that an editorial board meeting be arranged. Evidently the *Journal* liked the concept and agreed to meet with us at their office in New York City. They informed us that two editorial editors, an op/ed editor and a health reporter would be at the session.

Our next step was to develop a set of talking points for the Annenberg representatives that cut to the heart of the issue. We knew that *The Wall Street Journal* would not tolerate any superfluous information, nor would they tolerate anything perceived as mere propaganda. Our case had to be made quickly and with sound reasoning.

Role-playing often helps prepare your client for any twists in the conversation, and the unexpected can be turned into the expected by judicious preparation. Playing the devil's advocate, we grilled the Annenberg people (it was decided that the program's director and a senior fellow would represent the program) with a list of potential questions, some of them containing controversy. They needed to be prepared for the worst.

We decided that only one of us would accompany them to New York for the editorial board meeting. After all, the majority of our work was completed. *The Wall Street Journal* did not want to interview us.

The Wall Street Journal's office, with its lofty lobby and picturesque setting, is surely an exciting place to do business. Within its walls emanates some of the most insightful, provocative news copy of the entire world. Located near the southern tip of Manhattan, the *Journal* oozes history and ambience. Once inside the editorial offices, we were greeted by a most impressive team of editors whose names read like Who's Who in the field of journalism. After introductions were made, the editorial board of *The Wall Street Journal* got down to business.

They wanted to know facts and figures about organ donations and recommendations to improve the situation. "Why," they asked, "was this a situation that needed to be brought to the public's attention?"

Apart from the factual information, which flowed smoothly from the Annenberg representatives, our client provided a series of anecdotes on the subject. These personal stories seemed to make an impression. The tone of the meeting was so cordial that I didn't feel the need to make my presence felt. I felt proud when several tough questions presented during the course of the meeting were readily and skillfully answered by the Annenberg contingent. The role-playing had obviously helped.

Near the meeting's conclusion, the director of the program asked for the editorial board's support. This is imperative. You are there to ask for support of your agenda and that needs to be brought to the forefront at some point. Although no promises were made, an editorial appeared in the *Journal* a few weeks later supporting the Annenberg position.

At a statewide level, we once arranged a series of editorial board meetings with all of the major newspapers in Pennsylvania. The purpose was to request editorial support for the mission of the 93 private colleges and universities in the state, whose responsibilities and stewardship were being overshadowed by the often larger public universities and colleges.

Numerous editorials began to appear throughout the state endorsing the mission of private higher education. Like any other aspect of media relations, an editorial board meeting is only a good tactic to employ when the timing is right and you have an appropriate subject to present. Timing, preparation, and subject matter are everything.

News Conferences

Chief executive officers often are fond of news conferences. Reporters usually aren't. News conferences should be held for news of compelling interest and surpassing importance. If those criteria are not met, your president could be at the podium addressing one lonely staffer from the in-house newsletter (probably you) and no one else. CEOs don't enjoy that experience and neither will you.

A news conference can be an ego thing with company leaders who may get the feeling that if the President of the United States has them, why shouldn't they? For one reason, news conferences put you at the mercy of the news cycle. Even if you have a newsworthy announcement to make, the local TV and radio stations, as well as the newspapers, will weigh your news against the daily crush of events that, by definition, are news: fires, natural disasters, even sports events.

There was one instance when Dick Jones had all the local TV stations lined up to cover the kick-off for a major fund raising drive by a small Pennsylvania university. That day, however, the City of Philadelphia dropped a bomb on the headquarters of a militant group called MOVE. Suddenly there was no interest in a fund drive. In addition, news conferences tend to be local events, at best. They usually do not attract national reporters unless a reporter for the Associated Press happens to attend.

Two things that you can do when your CEO wants to speak with the media are:

- Send the information to reporters and say the CEO will be available from 10-11:30 a.m. if anyone wants to speak with him or her. This is a "media availability" rather than a "press conference."
- Bring the CEO to the media outlet for a one-on-one interview.

Using these tactics can insure some control over a news meeting.

Chapter

SIX

Target Marketing

Overall Markets

Target marketing entails narrowing one's focus to a specific publication or particular genre of news and channeling your energies in that direction. For example, you may have a source who is well versed in international trade issues. Surely, *The New York Times* covers this topic. But their coverage won't be as in-depth as a smaller publication like the *Journal of Commerce*. Founded in 1827, this daily became the first U.S. newspaper to publish a Chinese edition and has long been publishing special supplements devoted to the news of trade and economic developments in various Chinese cities. *The Journal of Commerce* was at one time widely read by members of Congress and lobbyists.

We would often spend days trying to contact a specific economic reporter from the major publications. On the other hand, a quick call to *The Journal of Commerce* in Washington or New York often resulted in a very nice placement – often known as a score – for our clients. We found that in the late 1980s and early 1990s, people at *The Journal of Commerce* were usually amenable to media sessions, which are visits by your source to a news outlet to meet directly with reporters and editors. Therefore, selecting a receptive and proper news outlet is a vital component for any national media campaign.

Although the *Journal of Commerce* has since ceased publication, a version continues to run on-line on the Web. Many similar lesser-known publications can score big for your national public relations campaign.

The reverse can also hold true. You can specifically target one major newspaper or magazine and hope to reap positive results through a calculated plan of attack.

Take the case of a professor of tax law from one small southern college who wanted her views on income taxes shared with the nation. We decided to target *Forbes Magazine* as a likely media outlet. Rather than send out countless news releases to all the major publications, a concentrated effort was focused on *Forbes*. First, back issues of *Forbes* were scanned in order to determine which reporters covered the topic of taxes in the past. With electronic search engines such as Lexus/Nexus and Dow Jones News Retrieval, this is easy to do these days. Next came the creation of a strong pitch letter, followed by phone calls to the selected reporters. A few months later the professor was featured in a 900-word article.

The odds are against anyone who tries to score with a national newspaper or broadcast outlet. It can and will happen for a public relations office that is highly organized and knows the proper guidelines. However, you may want to sometimes target your efforts at trade periodicals and journals or major metropolitan papers as opposed to national publications. The important thing is getting results for your institution or company. So what if all of your alumni or stockholders don't read the *Journal of Commerce* or *The Washington Times?* Reproducing such placements in alumni magazines and annual reports can certainly send positive messages to your alumni, stockholders and other constituents about the quality of your nonprofit or corporation.

One Professor of Russian from Colgate University, who eventually appeared in virtually every major news publication and on most national broadcast outlets, got her start by writing an article for *Foreign Affairs* – one of America's premier quarterlies. Widely read by those inside the Washington beltway, *Foreign Affairs* is the type of magazine that can propel someone into the national spotlight.

Marketing Your Story

Marketing a story through personal contact with reporters is always the preferred method of pitching any possible story idea. This entails a great amount of time and effort, which translates into money for a small public relations department. Any time spent away from the normal daily responsibilities must be calculated as an investment, since time is money.

For many small **PR** departments, this simply isn't feasible. A national media campaign means sacrificing too many other aspects of the job that demand constant attention, such as writing local and hometown news releases, arranging photo shoots, attending committee meetings, overseeing the in-house company newsletter and all other publications, fielding calls from the regional media, developing an ad campaign and supervising special events. It's often these internal demands that force many small public relations shops to hire consultants for a national media campaign.

Let's go back to Babson's former president, Bill Glavin. Previously a top executive with Xerox, Mr. Glavin was certainly well versed in the area of finances and how they affect the running of a college. Furthermore, he was willing to do media sessions – and he does them very well. Whether in New York talking to *The Wall Street Journal* or in Washington preparing for a national talk show appearance, Mr. Glavin was an energized, articulate spokesman for his college, continually bringing positive exposure to Babson. Alumni pride swelled at Babson during Mr. Glavin's tenure as president. And there's no doubt that he brought with him a sense of purpose concerning national publicity. Evidently his corporate background instilled in him the value of national publicity and its importance for a company's mission.

However, there are instances when media sessions with national reporters don't work out quite as well as you may have envisioned. One college president met for hours with an education reporter from *The New York Times* over an extended lunch to talk about the need for colleges to conduct capital campaigns. From an observer's vantage point, everything went extremely well. The president of the college later walked the streets of Manhattan beaming with thoughts of an anticipated feature in the hallowed *New York Times* on the worthiness of his institution's capital campaign. Not until four months later did the story run -- a front page *Sunday Times* one at that – but the president received only a one line mention that incorrectly stated the campaign's goal by 100 million dollars. We immediately called the *Times* and requested a correction, which they did. But this example illustrates the vicissitudes associated with national media relations. Certain things are beyond your control.

Gehrung Associates pioneered the concept of media sessions for college presidents and faculty, and the concept remains a staple in their national campaigns. Other national media relations firms also arrange media sessions for their corporate clients. In fact, it can be argued that arranging a media session for a corporate client with a national business or financial reporter is easier and less time consuming than arranging one for someone in higher education.

The reason seems to be that national publications and broadcast outlets expend far more effort into coverage for business and financial issues than they do for higher education. Thus, there are numerous reporters covering the business beat, and perhaps one or two (if it's a major news outlet) devoted to education. This is especially pertinent for those public relations people within the health care industry. Poll after poll indicates that first and foremost the reading or viewing public wants information about health.

Most national papers and networks recognize this fact and devote the appropriate personnel power needed to cover the wide array of health topics. In fact, so specialized is this field that reporters are normally divided into two beats: health and medical. And because so much ink and verbiage is given to these topics, it's usually a lot easier to find a health reporter to pitch a story to than it is to find someone covering higher education.

Executing Media Sessions

The idea of media sessions is simple, but the execution is often difficult. Learning to persevere and having thick skin are highly valued personality traits for anyone wishing to arrange media sessions with national reporters or assignment editors. They are busy people who may not tolerate intrusions. The success rate for arranging a media session is usually about five percent, but that low figure can mean huge results.

Knowing your topic very well and being prepared to convey it within a minute or less are sage bits of advice for media sessions. By narrowing your focus, you'll be able to concentrate on a specific issue and selected reporters. Remember, it doesn't matter to reporters if you're calling to have them meet with the CEO of Johnson & Johnson or the president of Harvard. You must have a topic that's timely or filled with controversy. Of course, most companies and colleges shy away from the latter. There are exceptions, and a CEO like Bill Gates will always attract a national media audience wherever he goes, no matter the timing or the topic.

The "platform" on which your source stands – what he or she has to say – is what sells a media session. The very fact that your client is a CEO is not by itself a door opener. Always develop "talking points" for your client to use on media visits.

Trend or roundup stories are a good way to pitch a media session for your expert if he or she happens to be truly well versed in the topic.

Pending books is another. Also, a major announcement such as a new product, a research center or an interesting new course may catch the attention of a reporter. Once again, research seems to be the operative word. Different and exciting research is a good way to open doors.

Whatever you decide to pitch, a phone call is the preferable way to make contact with a reporter. Studies have shown that news releases go virtually unnoticed, with faxes also having little effect. And unsolicited e-mail is not always welcome. That leaves phone calls. We will often write first and inform a particular reporter that we will be calling in a week. This seems to work well for us. As stated earlier, make sure that a specific reporter is still covering a particular issue.

Never call reporters to tell them that you happened to see their story on minorities in education, and that your college has the right person to comment on such a topic. It's too late! That story is finished. Try to anticipate trends ahead of time. If you happen to connect with the desired reporter, keep your pitch concise and to the point. For example, you might want to say, "I represent Such and Such Company. Our president will be in New York next week to address the National Association of Widget Makers on the topic of proposed government regulations. She has some strong opinions about the government's proposal. I know you've covered the topic before and thought you might be interested in meeting with her for a few minutes that day." That's all you need to say. If your expert has recently written a book or paper on the subject, then so much the better.

Furthermore, never leave a message for a national reporter requesting a return call; they're too busy. Be persistent and make the initial, personal contact. If personal contact seems impossible, leave a brief voice message explaining that a "backgrounder" (a detailed summary of the topic) is in the mail.

It's wise to try and arrange a number of media sessions during the same day in case a certain reporter fails to show for the meeting. This will invariably happen, even though you've confirmed the time and place ahead of time. At least with several media sessions, the day's not a total waste.

You might wonder whether or not the public relations director should accompany the client to the media session. In almost all cases the answer is "yes." National reporters can be abrupt and won't be afraid to attack if they smell blood. For example, one highly regarded professor of business from a small New England college strutted into *The New York Times* one day for a meeting with a seasoned columnist. After a grueling 45-minute session, which included attacks on his very thesis by the columnist, the professor staggered out of the office looking for a standing eight count. This treatment is unusual, but it can happen. If so, a savvy public relations person can often deflect some of the verbal attack by prudent interjection. The trick is to know the president's or faculty member's area of expertise and steer the conversation back into more friendly territory.

And you also need to know enough to stay out of the way when things are proceeding well. You are not there to show the reporter how much you know about the topic. Silence can be golden. One time during an editorial board meeting with *The Wall Street Journal,* an overly anxious, aggressive public relations consultant kept interrupting the flow of the conversation between his client and the editorial board. A frustrated editor finally asked the company's CEO, "Are you here to talk about numbers and facts or have your PR guy serve as your mouthpiece?" Needless to say, it proved to be a very embarrassing moment for the media consultant and the CEO.

Of course, the ability to think on one's feet is the true test for any good public relations director, something all national media consultants are trained to do well. Once during a media session in Washington, DC with a college president, a consultant demonstrated the ultimate form of thinking on one's feet. When pressed by the president on other methods of attaining national publicity, a quick witted, even-keeled media consultant calmly replied, "white paper." He went on to explain to the president that a white paper filled with charts, graphs and predictions, could attract the attention of some national reporters. Later, in confidence, he admitted having no clue of what to say for a brief second after being asked the question.

A few weeks later, the consultant's colleague was pressed for an answer regarding the same question: How can we get more national publicity? Having exhausted all of the usual options, the consultant quickly blurted out the words: "white paper." Several months later, two white papers were produced, both of them receiving scattered national exposure.

If arranging a media session seems impossible, you can always market a story through the traditional means – sending out a backgrounder to specific reporters. A backgrounder tends to be written in a feature style with anecdotal information included, as opposed to bland news releases. Be sure that all contact names, along with work and home phone numbers, are contained in the backgrounder.

Pitch Letters

A pitch letter is generally shorter than a backgrounder and geared more directly to a specific reporter. As such, a pitch letter is more personal. For example, you might want to write: "I've enjoyed your recent coverage of the Senate's proposed budget cuts, and thought you might be interested in seeing Dr. Smith's research on the topic." You can then briefly describe the research in a paragraph, indicating afterwards that additional information can be obtained by contacting you. Pitch letters should not be sent out in bulk. Target a few selected reporters and make sure they are the current people on the beat. This can't be emphasized enough. Knowing which reporters cover which beat is perhaps the most important ingredient of any national media relations plan. Stay current. We literally begin our day by scanning most of the national newspapers in order to determine who's covering which areas.

Obviously, a catchy first sentence for any pitch letter is a must. If you don't grab a reporter's attention immediately, you're finished. One mid-Atlantic school used, "In between flashing the hit and run sign, Coach James also has to use his cell phone to check in with the probation office," as the beginning of a pitch letter which eventually drew calls from three national reporters. The information went on to describe some of the unusual jobs held by coaches at small colleges. Coach James was a full-time probation officer.

On the next page you'll find an example of a pitch letter that resulted in a call back from a reporter for the *Wall Street Journal*, and eventually a placement in that prestigious newspaper.

Joseph Boyce
Senior Editor
The Wall Street Journal
200 Liberty Street
New York, NY 10281

Dear Mr. Boyce:

Leadership can be taught. That's the premise of the new Jepson
School of Leadership Studies at the University of Richmond.

With the Jepson School, Richmond becomes the first college or university to offer a degree in leadership.

To be sure, leadership education has its critics, the most common
complaint being: "Isn't leadership one of the qualities we expect a normal
liberal arts education to instill?" The question was debated loud and long
by U of R faculty. There are still skeptics.

Nonetheless, the first class offered by the Jepson School –
Foundations of Leadership – began this year with around 100 students
enrolled in the various sections.

"One definition of leadership is the capacity to work together with
others to achieve mutual goals," says Howard T. Prince, dean of the Jepson
School. "We have what might be described as a moral concept of leadership."

The Jepson School – founded with a $20 million gift from Robert S.
Jepson, Jr. – seeks to combine information about leadership into a whole.

"Knowledge and theories from all relevant fields will be combined
with experiences and programs to foster leadership capacities," says Dean
Prince. "A continual effort to relate theory and practice, reflection and
action, information and personal development, will characterize the educational philosophy of the Jepson School."

Dean Prince was head of the department of behavioral sciences and
leadership at West Point before coming to Richmond. The other faculty
members are:

Dr. James MacGregor Burns, Pulitzer Prize winning biographer of FDR
and author of "Leadership," an early call for leadership education.

Dr. Joanne Ciulla, formerly senior fellow at Penn's Wharton School. Ethics
and the philosophy of work are among her interests.

Dr. William Howe, a teacher in prep schools in the U.S. and abroad, is
now finishing his Ph.D. in education at Stanford.

According to Dean Prince, about 500 colleges and universities offer
something in the area of leadership education. In most cases, it's a course
or two, sometimes a co-curricular activity.

> If you are interested in the topic of teaching leadership, please let us know. We can provide a great deal of additional information about the Jepson School. Or call Dean Prince at xxx-xxxxx.
>
> Please let us know if there is anything further we can provide. We assist the University of Richmond with some public affairs work.

There are several points to be made here. First, the pitch letter is sent to a real person who was identified as someone who may be interested in the subject. This was determined through our research.

Second, the lead sentence is direct and captures the essence of the entire pitch in a few words as possible. Also, the letter offers some quotes. It's important to include quotes from the main players in order to demonstrate that these people have something important to say. The letter does include the fact that not everyone agrees with the program. This shows the reporter that there is an element of controversy involved and doesn't portray the program as perfect. You can't always try to convince national reporters that a program or project has no flaws. They'll see through it in a second. Don't be afraid to include both the pros and cons of the program within your pitch letter.

On the other hand, does this approach risk having some negative press included if indeed the story does appear in print? Possibly, but a positive overall tone of a story far outweighs any aspects that may contain some controversy. Of course, the backgrounds of everyone involved are included in the pitch letter to add an air of credibility to it. Finally, the expert's phone number is included in the event the reporter wants to contact that person directly.

Readability

One of the often overlooked elements of a good pitch letter is its readability. Would you rather scan something that's easy to read or do you prefer to slog through dense thickets of jargon and 75-word sentences? Remember that you have seven seconds to capture the attention of editors or producers with your pitch letter. After you have grabbed them you can still lose them by making them work too hard to read the letter. It's human nature. We prefer the easy road to the hard one. Make it easy on reporters by writing something that's easy to read. Many computer programs now have readability indexes. Essentially they reward short words and short sentences and they penalize long words and long sentences.

For years, we have used a formula that approximates the grade level a person should have reached to be able to read a document and understand it. If a document has a readability level of 12, for example, a senior in high school should be able to grasp it adequately. If you write something and it has an index of 18, however, you should go back and trim words and add periods to your run-on sentences.

If you don't have a computer program, here's a formula you can use by hand (which is still the way we do it) to determine a "fog index."

1) Use a sample of at least 250 words.
2) Find the percentage of big words – those with three syllables or more. Don't count proper names, three syllable words ending in "ed" or "es" or those that have been formed from shorter words, such as rattlesnake. Record the percentage of big words as a whole number (21, not .21).
3) Find the average sentence length in words by counting the number of words and dividing the total by the number of sentences.
4) Add the numbers you found in steps two and three. Multiply the sum by 0.4. Drop everything after the decimal point and you have the fog index.

The fog index roughly corresponds to the number of years of schooling you need to read the writing sample comfortably. An index of 16 supposedly means you need four years of college.

The important thing for writers to remember is that even well educated readers prefer stories with a low fog index. If you make a reader struggle you will lose him or her unless that person is intensely interested in the topic. Writing something that's easy to read is not the same as "dumbing down" your prose. We've been told, for example, that J.D. Salinger's classic "The Catcher in the Rye" has a readability index of six.

Broadcast Markets

The national broadcast markets offer unparalleled exposure for an institution but present challenges that are often out of one's grasp. The best way for a small institution or relatively unknown company to attain national TV visibility is to get big print visibility first, then leverage it by sending tear sheets of the article and making follow-up phone calls to assignment editors. Although the assignment editor has become a bit more tabloid sized these days, it's still possible to receive positive news coverage by aiming for the morning news shows.

Network affiliated shows like ABC's "20/20" often need some sort of expert to validate a story, while general news shows like to include an expert right on the back of the news. Talking heads from the academic field are often used on top of breaking news to comment on, say, Social Security, while CEOs and other top business officials are always needed on such programs as "Business Unusual" (CNN), "The News with Brian Williams" (MSNBC) or the "Fox News Channel."

Be sure your plan includes such broadcast outlets as ESPN if indeed you represent someone who has a particular slant on sports. For example, a rather industrious professor of finance at one midwestern university developed a formula that compared the salaries of today's athletes to those of the Babe Ruth era. We pitched him to not only The *Wall Street Journal* and *Fortune Magazine*, but to ESPN as well. He received a three-minute segment and became an instant celebrity on campus. The point is there are many national outlets available to you if you take the time to do your homework.

Don't neglect your local news since national outlets sometimes work through local affiliates, using feeders once a day. One of our clients, a medium-sized health care system in the east, has a wound care center that often uses cutting edge technology in order to heal wounds faster than the usual rate. Knowing that the local NBC affiliate would be interested in this, we called the health beat reporter at the local station and pitched her the story. Like all health features, we knew that we needed a patient to offer testimony as verification of the healing process.

This is another important point to keep in mind. You need to know what elements will make a good story even better. Health beat reporters love having a patient available for a story. This adds credibility from a viewer's perspective. They think, "Wow, if that works for her, then it may work for me." This approach tends to personalize the story for the viewer.

Our wound care story featured the latest methods of treating wounds within the comfort of the patient's home using a procedure known within the field as VAX. The patient, an affable, elderly gentleman, was perfect for the part and spoke from the heart about his positive experience. The three-minute segment aired locally a few days later. It impressed the network powers-to-be so much that NBC sent it out over their national feed the next day, making it available to hundreds of NBC affiliates throughout the country. We received reports from New York City, Los Angeles and Orlando that it aired in their markets. Calls to the wound care center came in from similar centers across the country wanting to know more about the procedure. Suddenly, the hospital was known nationally. Additional details of working with the broadcast media will be outlined fully in Chapter seven, "Success With the Broadcast Media."

With the success of CNN and the abundance of other cable outlets, the demand for talking heads has increased greatly over the past decade, and it's wise to discover which assignment editor handles which beat for CNN. Many assignment editors at CNN are aggressive story-seekers, and they have been known to welcome media sessions with the appropriate source.

Likewise, C-SPAN has become a good source for talking heads with their morning viewer call-in show, and will, on occasion, visit your site to air a speech if the topic is timely and the speaker is prominent. Newton Minow, the former FCC chairman, once said that he received more phone calls from friends, colleagues and well wishers as the result of an appearance on C-SPAN than he did after being interviewed on "CBS This Morning."

Handling Media Requests

Every now and then a reporter from the national media contacts you to find a source for a story. Assuming that the reporter wants something that will reflect positively on your institution and its leaders – or at least the story will be neutral in impact – you will want to try your best to respond. If you do, you will find you are contacted more often.

As you build contacts and trust among the national media, you can expect media requests. One of your goals should be to get your experts listed directly into the address books of influential reporters. Your hope is that whenever there is a news story that intersects with your client's area of expertise, the reporters call your clients immediately.

Numerous political scientist experts represented by Dick Jones Communications now simply call us to say that "I was interviewed by ABC Radio about the Iowa Caucus," or some similar political event. This reflects a level of trust between the source and the journalist, and the process often begins with effective handling of media requests.

Whether you represent a college, a trade association, a hospital, a plumbing supply company, an insurance firm, a steel mill or an Internet dot.com startup, your employees – particularly your senior employees – have expertise to share that would be of interest to the general public. When they share it, your institution is positioned as a "player" on the national scene.

Media requests usually come by phone or e-mail, the latter increasingly being the vehicle of choice. They can be vague – "I need someone to talk about car insurance," or specific – "I need someone to tell me why car insurance rates were higher in Massachusetts than in Pennsylvania for the same makes of cars during 1998."

When responding to media requests, keep one simple rule in mind: give the reporter more reasons to say "yes" to your source than to say "no." We have seen first-hand how individual PR directors use and misuse this rule. Were we to get a media request from a reporter at the Associated Press or from a business-desk reporter in New York saying, "I need someone to talk about car insurance," we would pass it along to the PR directors at the clients we serve. Some would drop the ball. Others would put it into play.

Some PR directors would simply give us a name. "Call Professor Sarah Smith at 123- 555-7890." This is inadequate. Who is Professor Smith? What is her title? Why should the reporter call her? A response like this gives a reporter too many opportunities to refuse.

Others would identify Smith as a professor of insurance and real estate. Better, but still inadequate. Why should the journalist call Smith over any other source? A much better response is, "Call Sarah Smith, professor of insurance and real estate, at 123-555-7890. She's done three journal articles in the past two years on inter-state comparisons of car insurance rates."

You see the pattern? The journalist often has to sell sources to editors. He needs validation that he's going to be spending his valuable time talking with someone who can help to advance the story.

But even this effort can and should be topped to ensure that the journalist will speak with your source. Best of all would be a response like this: "Call Sarah Smith, professor of insurance and real estate, at 123-555-7890 (office) or 123-555-8901 (home). Her e-mail address is: smith@ins.edu. She has written three journal articles in the last two years on inter-state comparison of car insurance rates. 'Demographics and population density play a key role in determining auto insurance rates,' she says. 'The pattern is very clear over the last 25 years.' I've spoken with her and she'll be in her office until 3 p.m. today. She's leaving for a conference tomorrow but does check her e-mail when she's on the road."

This response will get the job done. The journalist has all the facts needed to make a decision on whether to call Professor Smith and the decision will probably be "yes."

The elements of success for responding to media requests include:

- Your source's name.
- Your source's exact title.
- How best to reach your source and when he or she is available. If possible, give office and home phone numbers and e-mail address.
- Information on what makes your source an expert.
- A quote from your source, if possible.

The handling of media requests reveals a fundamental reality about national media relations. The more work you put into it, the greater your likelihood of success will be. There is no way around that hard truth.

A number of "play for pay" sites have emerged on the Internet and some of them are useful, depending on what sort of clients you repre-sent. College and university PR people are familiar with "Profnet" (www.profnet.com) a service run by PR Newswire whereby journalists post queries to PR offices. Schools pay PR Newswire for the privilege of belonging to "Profnet" and the rates are based on a school's enrollment. Since hundreds of schools belong to Profnet, successful use of the serv-ice depends on an institution's ability to monitor it closely and respond quickly.

"Newswise" (www.newswise.com) is another Internet service target-ed to benefit journalists covering selected fields such as medicine, sci-ence, business, pop culture and education. Organizations pay Newswise"for the privilege of uploading stories, which then are made available to journalists covering those beats. The Darwinian rules of journalism dominate this realm as they do all others. Interesting stories stand a chance of getting noticed. Dull stories don't. Like Profnet, Newswise is also a place where journalists post media requests.

Since national media relations tasks are labor-intensive activities, you will want to maximize the impact of the work you do. When you interview a source such as Professor Smith to get information for a media request, be thinking of what else you can do with that information. After the AP reporter writes the story – and includes Professor Smith and her institution in it – the information gathered by the PR director might also be used to interest other media outlets in doing their own stories. Or you may have uncovered a story for the school or company magazine.

Get a reputation for handling media requests well, and it will pay off in increased trust from journalists and more national coverage. Your institution's sources will be "in the Rolodex" and that's where you want them to be.

Don't Believe It Until You've Seen It In Print

Perhaps the most frustrating part of working with the national media is the fact that so many things are beyond your control when trying to land a placement. You can do everything right and still have no results with the national media to show for all your hard work.

But you must forge ahead. The old adage, "Nobody knows what I do until I stop doing it," is certainly true for those of us involved with national publicity efforts. If your company or client has become accustomed to national publicity, ceasing such efforts is akin to removing the water coolers during the summer. It becomes a necessity that's hard to live without.

There will be times you'll feel certain that you've landed a national placement, only to have it never materialize. This can happen for a variety of reasons.

The scenario goes like this. You've identified your story, developed it and targeted it for *U.S. News and World Report.* You've met with the education reporter at the Washington, D.C. offices. You brought along a professor of educational psychology who recently completed a major research project that outlines reasons why charter elementary schools won't be successful in the U.S. The topic is hot and the education reporter readily accepted your request for a personal interview with the professor.

You brief the professor ahead of time and prepare her for all kinds of possible questions that the education reporter may ask. By the way, you also arranged additional media sessions throughout the day with other news outlets. But it was *U.S. News* that expressed the most interest initially.

All goes well during the interview. Even the education reporter, a hard-to-read type of reporter, appears genuinely impressed with the professor's research. He explains that the article he's working on will run "in two months." He further states that he needs to fill in substantial holes and that this research should help nicely. "Will the professor be willing to sit for a photo?" he inquires. They exchange business cards as we leave. The professor and I stop at a small, outdoor café near *U.S. News* and congratulate one another for the fine job we both did. We couldn't be happier.

I'm not worried that the education reporter didn't call the professor in the time leading up to the article. After all, he had gathered a lot of material during the 70-minute interview with the professor. When the article appears as scheduled, there is no mention of the professor or her research. There is extensive copy concerning the research of a professor at another university.

The professor is devastated. It's a cruel lesson, but not an uncommon one as far as national media relations is concerned. Reporters have several sources, and they can't quote each one. Also, some reporters have a pre-conceived idea of what their story will look like and will search out information that best supports this premise.

Getting the Most from Special Interest Periodicals

Not all national publications, be they newspapers or magazines, are written with a general audience in mind. Those magazines that are general in scope include the big three – *Time, Newsweek* and *U.S. News & World Report.* Newspapers that serve a general audience include *The New York Times, USA Today,* and the *Washington Post.* It can be argued that *The Wall Street Journal* is more a trade publication, geared to a more specialized audience than a newspaper for the general public, although it battles *USA Today* for the title of "nation's highest circulation newspaper." Either way you view *The Wall Street Journal,* its prestige and large circulation make it one of the most influential papers in the world.

Your national media relations campaign should always include special interest publications as an integral part of the plan. Do not underestimate the significance of these publications. Just because you may not read these journals doesn't mean that they don't carry great influence in selected pockets of the corporate and nonprofit world.

In fact, many of these periodicals are the "Bibles" of the industry they serve. A perfect example is the *Chronicle of Higher Education*. The title itself may not ring a bell in the minds of the general public. And surely its circulation is limited in scope to colleges and universities throughout the world. However, the *Chronicle* is "must" reading for anyone involved with higher education. To place a client in the *Chronicle* is definitely a coup for the public relations director. And often that professor or college president who is quoted or featured will receive more feedback from colleagues than if the article had appeared in *USA Today.*

In addition to its influence on college campuses, the *Chronicle of Higher Education* is also referenced frequently in *The New York Times* and *Washington Post*, among others. If a reporter from *The New York Times* highlights an educational issue that involves statistics – such as salaries of professors or college presidents – then it's likely they will gather this data from the *Chronicle* and reference the publication appropriately. Therefore, it is the responsibility of all public relations directors who work for a college or university to make inroads with the *Chronicle of Higher Education.*

Editors at the *Chronicle* are fond of saying that their employer is "*The Chronicle of Higher Education*," not "*The Chronicle for Higher Education*." In other words, they are not cheerleaders for any college. You must approach them as you would any other media outlet and this is good advice for approaching special interest publications in all fields.

In reality, the circulation numbers for special interest journals are relatively insignificant as far as national media relations is concerned. If you determine through conversation with those within the industry itself that a certain trade journal is considered important, then by all means add that to your media list.

Bill Glavin's background as a Xerox executive prior to coming to Babson College as its president served as fodder for a very significant placement in *Industry Week*, a highly regarded publication that provides those in the business sector with timely, factual information. Most CEOs read the journal religiously. For corporate executives, having a feature in *Industry Week* about themselves or their company is a worthy accomplishment that is widely noticed by peers.

Knowing the importance attached to *Industry Week*, I included it as part of a national media relations plan for Mr. Glavin of Babson. Prior to contacting the appropriate reporter at *Industry Week*, I had to do my homework. Since I was not entirely familiar with this trade journal, it was necessary for me to pull several back issues and review their content, tone, style and masthead. It was clear from the reporting throughout the publication that *Industry Week* took an intimate look at the inner sanctums of the business world itself. One reporter in particular stood out as someone who might be interested in speaking with Mr. Glavin. He had written several human interest stories on prominent CEOs, each with a touch of adventure and risk. As far as I could tell, the reporter had never featured either Xerox or higher education in his reporting. I reasoned that he might enjoy talking with someone as worldly as Mr. Glavin.

As it turned out, the reporter was one of the friendliest, approachable reporters to be found. The very first question you should ask of a national reporter is, "Do you have a minute or are you on deadline?" It lets them know that you're aware of their tight schedule. Although this reporter was normally very busy, he always seemed to have time to talk about a potential story. Likewise, he was agreeable to media sessions. Right from the start, he expressed a high level of interest in the Bill Glavin story, and he readily agreed to meet with Mr. Glavin and me at his Washington, D.C. office.

During the interview, both the reporter and Mr. Glavin seemed to develop a healthy respect for one another. The questions were pointed and open ended. The responses were informed and anecdotal. The result was a very provocative piece (excerpted below) in *Industry Week* for Babson.

Mr. Glavin Goes To Babson
By John S. McClenahen
Industry Week, July 1, 1991

Two years ago, in suburban Boston, a war marched in on William F. Glavin. During July and August of 1989, about 40 professors from the business and liberal arts faculties at Babson College, taking advantage of their new president's open-office policy, individually sat down with Mr. Glavin and launched some verbal volleys.

> . . .Bill Glavin listened for two months – and then decided he'd try to disarm the situation with a story . . . . The point Mr. Glavin was trying to make to the Babson faculty was that competition that counts is on the outside, not the inside. Babson was – and is – competing against other business schools – and not only those in the Northeast – for students, for financial and other resources, and for first-rate faculty.
>
> *Reprinted from Industry Week, © 1991. All rights reserved.*

Selecting Special Interest Periodicals

When dealing with both the national media and special interest periodicals, it's hard to generalize as to which reporters are most amenable when working with public relations people. However, major special interest journals give the impression that they are indeed more approachable.

It always makes good sense to understand if a special interest journal or periodical has a particular conservative or liberal "slant" to it before including it as part of your media relations plan. You certainly would want to proceed cautiously if your CEO or university president has the opportunity to appear in, say, *Insight Magazine* if he or she has opinions that are more to the left than the right.

Based in Washington, D.C., and a sister publication of the conservative *Washington Times, Insight* makes no bones about its right spectrum approach to journalism. But placements aren't out of the realm of possibility even if you don't agree with the philosophy behind the publication. After all, it's usually within the editorials where the biases appear, not within the text of the articles themselves. We have worked closely with *Insight* over the years, and we have successfully placed numerous articles here. Its education and science sections are well respected, and the reporters normally capture the essence of the story.

If by chance the story you are pitching to a national news outlet happens to contain several strong liberal messages, you'd probably be better suited to go after a publication such as the *New Republic*, which has long been dominant among the periodicals in terms of national and global commentary. As the "Media Guide" reports, "Its identity is with the

Democrats, and its more neoliberal than knee jerk, challenging the party line more often than elevating it."

Since special interest journals or certain periodicals may not reach as large a general audience as many of the news magazines, it is important to get the most out of your placements by including them in annual reports and student guides. In addition, send copies of these placements to your VIP list and always include the Board of Trustees.

Some special interest journals or periodicals to consider are: *Financial Times, Investor's Daily, The American Spectator, The Atlantic Monthly, Barron's, Defense News, The Economist, Financial World, Foreign Affairs, Harvard Business Review, The Nation, National Journal, National Review, The New Republic, Insight, The Spectator,* and *World Press Review.*

If you happen to be the director of communications for a company that makes Ferris Wheels, you would surely want to become familiar with trade journals such as *Amusement Business.* Did your firm build an innovative new headquarters? Maybe *Architecture* should hear about it. Do you manufacture gardening supplies? Pay attention to *National Gardening.* Almost all media guides contain information on trade journals. Familiarize yourself with all of the periodicals related to your particular industry.

Chapter

Seven

Success with the Broadcast Media

Ever since the day when households across the country flicked on the television for the first time, the debate has lingered over which news medium has the most significant impact on the news psyche of the American people. From the days of Edward R. Murrow to Walter Cronkite and Tom Brokaw, millions of people throughout the country have received their daily doses of news through television. Now such cable giants as CNN and CNBC have added to TV's power status.

There's no denying the enormous influence television news has on the American and global community. It's a medium that offers unparalleled exposure by making its way into virtually every household in the United States.

Regardless of your particular views on its merits, TV impacts society like no other medium. Its power is the reason why all presidential and other political candidates spend most of their campaign budgets on TV ad campaigns. And while the debate may linger forever about the impact and influence of TV news versus news printed in the newspapers, there's little doubt that you'll want to include the broadcast media prominently within your national media relations plan.

We often ask ourselves which medium produces the most visible results for the clients we serve. Is it TV with its global reach? Perhaps. Or is it national newspapers such as *The New York Times* with their storied history and renowned reporters? Well, we believe the answer is an emphatic, "that depends." It all comes down to the audience you're trying to reach.

For example, when we consulted for the Association of Independent Colleges and Universities of Pennsylvania, (AICUP) a non-profit organization that assists more than 80 private colleges and universities with lobbying efforts and development support, we needed to increase awareness of AICUP's research to both those in higher education and other decision makers.

We decided that the president of AICUP, Dr. Brian C. Mitchell, should play a major role in our national media relations campaign. Dr. Mitchell knew a good sound bite when he heard one, and he surely appeared to be able to offer one as well.

AICUP had just completed a two-year study that took an in-depth look at the graduation class of 1995 for the private colleges and universities throughout the Keystone State. The study detailed such things as the amount of debt these students had accumulated after their four or five years at a private college, and starting salaries of students entering the job market.

It was certainly not a unique study. Other states had conducted similar studies over the years. But we believed that since private colleges and universities in Pennsylvania educate over 220,000 students, the national media would view this particular study as a microcosm of higher education in general. Because we were trying to reach an audience of decision makers and those with a vested interest in higher education, such as parents, it seemed logical to market our story to national broadcast outlets that included National Public Radio and C-Span.

The methodology behind pitching a story to the national broadcast media is basically the same as to the national print media. You need a well-developed pitch letter followed by personal phone calls to selected reporters or people on the assignment desk. There is a slight difference. With the broadcast media, it may not be as apparent to whom you should pitch the story idea.

Scan the bylines of national papers and you'll know who covers which beats. You can call them directly. But with the national broadcast media, you won't be calling Larry King directly. Like all other anchors or talk show hosts, Larry King has his own staff of researchers and bookers. It's usually these bookers you need to target for talk shows and assignment editors for network news broadcasts. Of course, there are certain broadcast correspondents who cover special beats such as health, and they are often willing to hear directly from PR people who have a good story idea.

Pitching to the Right Person

Bruce D. Itule and Douglas A. Anderson describe positions in a broadcast newsroom:

News Writing and Reporting for Today's Media
by Bruce D. Itule and Douglas A. Anderson
© 1994, McGraw-Hill. Reprinted with permission of the
McGraw-Hill Companies

News Director: At the top of the newsroom is the news director, who reports to a station manager or general manager and does many of the jobs that a managing editor of a newspaper does. The news director is responsible for the entire news operation, including what goes on the air, the newsroom budget, and hiring and firing most reporters and other personnel. At larger stations there also is an assistant news director, who helps in the business and editorial areas and may be used in long-range planning of news coverage. In a typical television newsroom a number of people work under the news director to produce the television newscast.

Executive Producer: The executive producer runs the newsroom. He or she is responsible for story content, reading and editing reporters' scripts as they come in from the field. At a smaller station the executive producer may also make assignments and decide the layout of each news show.

Assignment Editor: Many stations have two assignment editors (or assignment managers), one working during the day and the other at night. They run the "desk," the reporters' contact with the newsroom. They coordinate all assignments, keep track of crews in the field, listen to police and fire radios, make follow-up calls for reporters and take incoming calls. At larger stations there also may be a planning editor working on the desk who is responsible for long-term planning of coverage of future events, such as trials or elections. This person also plans special projects such as series to be used during "sweeps" (ratings) periods and is responsible for specialty reporters who cover areas such as consumer, financial and medical news.

Broadcast Producers: These men and women put the newscasts together. If a station has newscasts at noon, 6 p.m. and 10 p.m., it may also have three broadcast producers. They are responsible for their own shows, choosing which stories to use, in what order to use them, how long to make them and what production style. They work closely with assignment editors to decide which reporters will cover which stories, and they work with the news director and executive producer to decide which stories will make it onto the air.

Associate Producer: Associate Producers help the broadcast producers lay out their news shows. There is usually one associate producer for each broadcast producer. If the station is a network affiliate, the associate producer will monitor the feeds.

When we want to contact the appropriate broadcast person, normally the booker, assignment editor, or producer, we don't rely solely on media guides that are readily available and ubiquitous in virtually all public relations offices. These guides can become outdated a few months after being published since producers or bookers within the broadcast profession tend to bounce around a bit or change positions altogether. In a pinch, they can serve a purpose such as providing a phone number, e-mail address or street address of a media outlet.

The guides can help you locate a particular reporter. But we also back this information up with a phone call to determine if that reporter is still covering that beat. Scanning the national papers each day will also help. But that's something you can't do for the broadcast outlets. Thus, media guides can assist you in your efforts to locate the proper booker for a talk show or assignment editor for a news program. Always confirm media guide information by making a phone call to the news outlet.

When we decided that National Public Radio would be our first choice for Dr. Mitchell of AICUP, we knew we had our work cut out for ourselves. NPR does not have the reputation of relying on those in the public relations profession for their news tips. NPR's program agenda is quite different from the other network broadcasts. Relatively speaking, they have a small cadre of reporters who seek out their own stories through a variety of sources. But they will not turn away a good story idea if it is presented to them properly.

We listened to NPR's national programming as often as possible in order to get a feel for the format of the various programs, and to ascertain which reporters might be interested in a story concerning higher education. We also called NPR's offices in Washington, DC and inquired whether or not they had a reporter who focused on education. We were told that would be Claudio Sanchez. We recognized the name from some of his news reports we had heard.

Once we identified NPR and Mr. Sanchez as our goal, we developed a pitch letter and sent it directly to Mr. Sanchez. We explained that the AICUP study was timely and important since it countered a number of highly publicized studies that showed college graduates having a hard time making ends meet. In fact, it directly challenged the premise of a Tom Brokaw NBC News report that summed up the job status of recent college graduates by referring to the line, "Do you want fries with your burgers?"

The AICUP report found that college graduates, at least from the private sector, were faring far better than was generally perceived. We thought NPR might be interested in hearing more. A week or two after our pitch letter, which referenced the "fries with burgers " line, Mr. Sanchez of NPR called us and wanted to hear more about the report. He expressed a genuine interest in the report and indicated he would like to talk directly with Dr. Mitchell of AICUP. We seized the opportunity and offered to have Dr. Mitchell come to Washington at Mr. Sanchez's earliest convenience. We arranged a meeting within two weeks.

Preparing Your Expert

Preparing someone to speak with a broadcast reporter is far different from preparing someone to talk with the print media. We knew going into the meeting with NPR that it would be a taped interview to be possibly (and we emphasize "possibly") aired at a later date. Since all broadcast journalists compile their reports by using sound bites of 30 seconds or less (usually much less), it is imperative that the interviewee be prepped to speak in this manner before the interview takes place.

We spent a good deal of time role playing with Dr. Mitchell by asking some very difficult questions that could be potentially used by NPR. We made sure he knew the detailed intricacies of the report (which he did) and also made sure that he answered succinctly. Dr. Mitchell was a natural and included appropriate anecdotes and humor in his responses.

It is very important when talking with the broadcast media to not come across as stiff or unprepared since that may be the 20 seconds they decide to air. The use of humor and anecdotes is a prudent use of time during the interview. Dr. Mitchell did a superb job. Evidently NPR agreed, and they aired a four-minute segment on the report by AICUP. Dr. Mitchell received congratulatory calls from colleagues across the country for weeks on end after the broadcast.

Newton Minow, with his extensive experience, was the best we've ever seen when speaking with the broadcast media. Prior to his "How Vast the Wasteland Now" speech on May 9, 1991, which revisited the state of affairs for TV 30 years to the date of his "The Vast Wasteland" speech of 1961, we assumed that NPR would be one of the broadcast outlets eager to talk with Mr. Minow. In addition, we would offer a pre-speech exclusive interview to one of the national broadcast affiliates.

Offering one broadcast an exclusive is not a strategy that those of us in the PR business can afford to employ too often. First of all, "exclusive" implies that the news is of major importance. We usually don't have that luxury. We normally have a story idea that has potential, not a sure thing like the Minow speech. And depending on the timing, it's often necessary to contact a number of national broadcasters at the same time and hope one of them bites.

The NPR interview was arranged via one phone call to the assignment editor who quickly recognized the opportunity to capture a moment of journalistic history. During the taped interview with NPR's Bob Edwards, Mr. Minow delighted the reporter with his experience, knowledge and humorous anecdotes.

Admittedly, not all clients have the name recognition of Newton Minow. But since he was recognizable, we knew we had to make the most of a good thing. We came to the conclusion that an "exclusive" interview with one of the major networks would be the best way to proceed. And to not anger any of the networks that we would have to work with in the future, we sent out classified letters to selected assignment editors at the morning shows of ABC, CBS, NBC and CNN. We had called each assignment editor beforehand to let him or her know that information about Mr. Minow's speech at Columbia University in New York City was forth coming.

We indicated in the letter that because of time constraints, Mr. Minow would only be able to appear on one network. And although this was true, we also believed that such a tactic would add a sense of urgency to the message.

A day after the letters were mailed, "CBS This Morning" called and booked Mr. Minow for a live interview with anchor Harry Smith the day of the speech. The interview went very smoothly, and it even included film from their archives of Mr. Minow's speech to the National Association of Broadcasters on May 9, 1961. Mr. Minow, who did not need any prior coaching, provided millions of viewers with an insightful recollection of an important piece of TV nostalgia.

Appearance Letter

The following letter is an example of the preparation and detail that should accompany any appearance on national TV:

Newton N. Minow
Director
The Annenberg Washington Program

Mr. Minow,

As scheduled, CBS This Morning will have a car waiting for you tonight at the airport when you arrive at 8:35 p.m. The name of the car company is Davel.

Tomorrow, the same car company will pick you up at the Regency at 7:15 a.m. and take you to CBS studios. Producer Judy Hole will greet you, and you are scheduled to appear somewhere between 8:05 and 8:25 for a 5 minute interview with Harry Smith.

If by chance something goes wrong, Judy Hole's home number is xxxxxxx and the CBS This Morning 24-hour hot line is xxxxxxx. Judy Hole's direct line at CBS is xxxxxxx. The car company's number is xxxxxxx. In case the car is not waiting for you in the morning – highly unlikely – please take a cab to the CBS This Morning studio on 530 W. 57th and enter near 11th Ave.

If your plans change tonight as far as your flight is concerned, please call the car company.

Good luck.

Details are extremely important when arranging a scheduled appearance on a live national talk show. You only have one opportunity to get it right. This is no time to take anything for granted.

Finding a News Hook

When Marywood University received word that it had been granted $10 million to create a Military Family Institute, we believed that it would be possible to pitch a story idea to the national broadcast media. Of course, we needed a strong news hook. The fact that the university received $10 million was insignificant in and of itself. It was our responsibility to find that news hook on which we could hang our pitch.

We researched past issues of *The Chronicle of Higher Education* in order to ascertain if any other colleges had something similar to a Military Family Institute. We discovered that although military issues were indeed being studied at a variety of colleges and universities, it seemed that none were looking at the type of issues being proposed at Marywood's Military Family Institute.

The one proposed research project that caught our attention was to look at the ratio of military personnel who had acquired a lot of bad debt. And although the project was two years from completion, we thought a major TV network might want to talk with officials at Marywood University prior to the project's inception. This is not normally the case, but we used the angle that the project could be introduced via the media and perhaps followed on a periodic basis throughout the course of the next two years.

Our pitch letter was sent to all four major news networks, ABC, CBS, NBC, and CNN, along with C-Span. A few weeks later ABC "World News Tonight" called and said they'd like to send a reporter to interview someone at the university. Since the Military Family Institute had not yet taken form, it appeared logical to have Sister Mary Reap, IHM, the president of the university, speak to the institute's future plans.

We knew that this interview would not be an easy one for the president since there were critics who called the $10 million "pork barrel" money from an influential Congressman. Indeed, *The Washington Post* reported as much in a scathing article. We felt the need to set the record straight, and perhaps ABC "World News Tonight" would provide that forum. We agreed it was worth the gamble.

If you have a client who is paranoid about speaking with any of the media for fear of words taken out of context or a reporter putting a negative slant on the story, then it's your job to convince them otherwise. Unless you have an op/ed published, there's always the chance that an article or TV sound bite might not appear exactly the way you want it to.

As national media consultants, we spend a good deal of our time outlining the positive aspects of having an article in a national paper. We tell our clients that for the most part, if a story idea is pitched to the national media, we will make certain that we only provide those elements that are truly positive. If we do our job properly, the reporter will want to highlight those positive attributes within the article. Might a little bit of controversy slip in? Certainly. But that should never overshadow the overall, positive theme of the story.

The ABC "World News Tonight" interview with Sister Mary Reap of Marywood University is a good example. We knew that the reporter might attempt to back Sister Mary into a corner about the so-called "pork" money. And we spent hours prepping her for those types of questions. We all agreed that by allowing ABC to come to campus and preparing properly for the interview, the positive results would far out-weigh the potential downsides. A story about Marywood University on national TV would propel the university into the national spotlight. It might even increase admission applications.

We also had complete confidence in Sister Mary's ability to answer the tough questions, and we knew that she could put a positive spin on questions asked of her. As predicted, the ABC reporter did ask about the large grant and its implications of "pork." However, Sister Mary was up to the task and explained that without government support, most important research being conducted at our nation's universities would be impossible. The entire segment ran for only 45 seconds on ABC, but everyone at the university believed it was well worth the effort.

Leveraging Print Media to Get Broadcast Attention

You can also use success with the print media to attain national coverage with one of the networks. This strategy worked particular well for Eckhard Pfeiffer of Compaq Computer Corporation.

It was only after a number of placements in such publications as *USA Today, The New York Times* and *Christian Science Monitor* that we decided to land some national broadcast interviews for Mr. Pfeiffer. CNNfn was a natural place to begin since the cable news network concentrates almost exclusively on business related topics. As with the print media, don't limit yourself to the big three or four networks. CNNfn, C-Span, MSNBC and others offer a wide array of good options for your national media relations campaign.

Once again, it was time for us to seek out and review the various programs on CNNfn in order to determine which ones would be most receptive to an interview with the CEO of a major computer company. However, it's not enough just to offer the network the CEO of Compaq as a guest. Regardless of the CEO, you must have a news angle that is attractive to the media. Don't merely pitch the fact that Eckhard Pfeiffer will be in town. You'll lose all your credibility with the media. And in this business, credibility is everything.

We knew that Compaq was about to introduce a new desktop product that may change the way people use computers, and surely Mr. Pfeiffer would be able to discuss this with CNNfn. The new product would be our news hook. Steve Young, host of CNNfn's "Digital Jam," looks at technology products and markets; he would probably be interested in having Mr. Pfeiffer appear to talk about not only Compaq's new desktop product, but also the future of Compaq in general.

Making the Phone Call

Once again, the operative word is "research." It's literally impossible for any public relations consultant to be current with each and every broadcast opportunity and/or on air talent. Only through time-consuming research that involves scanning both the cable channels and media guides are national media consultants able to determine which broadcast options exist for their clients. We recommend the "News Media Yellow Book" which can be purchased by calling 212-627-4140.

Prior to calling CNNfn, I developed a short list of talking points that would help me make my pitch in a succinct manner. This strategy is very important, whether you're calling the national broadcast or print media. Once you reach the designated reporter or assignment editor, you cannot ramble on forever about the merits of your client.

As with any good pitch letter, you need to capture the interest of the reporter or assignment editor within the first few seconds of your call. Remember, these are very busy people who don't have time to listen to a public relations person spout off about why this story is "too important" to be passed over. The assignment editor or reporters themselves will decide that once you've conveyed the essential elements and news hook of the proposed story.

When I called CNNfn to try and reach the assignment editor of Digital Jam, it was Steve Young himself who answered. He was based in New York City where the show aired, and he explained that he often booked his own guests.

In addition to the host or assignment editor, you can try and reach an associate producer, segment producer or senior producer. In the case of smaller networks, the same person often wears all of these hats. Not so with the major networks. And because so many production people are involved with a news show, it is very important to narrow down your contacts before making your pitch call.

Initially try and reach the assignment editor. You may learn that a segment or associate producer actually books interviews. If so, keep track of that information so you'll be ready the next time you call that network.

Knowing when to call is as important as knowing whom to call, and this is equally as important for the print media. These reporters all work around deadlines, and it is essential that the public relations person knows what criteria to follow before picking up the phone. A general rule of thumb is to call members of the national media early, preferably first thing in the morning. We like to come in to work around 7:30 a.m. and begin making phone calls to selected reporters in order to pitch story ideas. You may very well end up talking to an answering machine, but that's OK. If your pitch is interesting enough, these reporters will call you back for additional information on the topic. A large percentage of our placements result from a reporter's call back.

And don't worry if your call isn't returned within the hour or even during the same day. We've had reporters call us back weeks after our initial pitch. They work according to their own schedule, not yours. But they will call back if they think you have a good story for them. That's why it's very important to write down some key points you want to make before calling these reporters. You don't want to leave a rambling, incoherent message. Be succinct.

There are exceptions to the early morning call. Assignment editors who work for national broadcast shows that air during the morning hours, such as the "Today Show," are too busy with the show to respond to your calls in the morning. Wait until early afternoon to call these editors.

You may be nervous before your first call to a national reporter. That's only natural. After all, if this is your first attempt at attaining national publicity, the territory is foreign to you. Not only should you have prepared notes on what to say, but practice saying these things to yourself before making the call. You'll find this can relieve some of the anxiety of speaking with a national reporter for the first time.

"Hello, I represent Compaq Computer Corporation." In this instance, it was imperative to mention "Compaq" as quickly as possible because of its high name recognition. This was not as important when we represented Marywood University since the school was not a nationally recognized institution. The story idea itself was always first and foremost. It turned out that CNNfn was about to run a series of shows on the future of the personal PC, and Mr. Young said our timing couldn't have been any better. He would interview Mr. Pfeiffer as his first guest for the series. Serendipity can play a role in any national media relations campaign. However, it's usually skill, knowledge of the media, and resolve that lead to desired results.

Structuring Your Story Idea and Interview

When working with the TV broadcast media, it is especially important to outline the proposed story idea in a manner that includes an opportunity for visuals. After all, TV is a visual medium, and without the option to include some interesting visuals as part of the story, your pitch to the producers will fall far short. We offered CNNfn some B-Roll (film already shot that complements a news story) of consumers buying computers off store shelves. Normally the networks have all the stock footage they need, and B-Roll is certainly not a necessary element of a national media relations campaign. However, the opportunity to allow the network to film some visually stimulating aspects of the story at your site can enhance your pitch.

The CNNfn interview with Mr. Pfeiffer was to be a live, four or five minute segment. At our request, Mr. Young agreed to provide Mr. Pfeiffer with a list of questions he might be asking during the segment. It is always prudent to ask the interviewer if he or she can furnish a list of potential questions so your client won't be caught off guard during a live interview. You'll find that some are willing to oblige, while others prefer that the interview be conducted cold without any preparation.

Regardless of the interviewer's reluctance to supply a list of potential questions, you can get a feel for what tone and direction the interview will take by asking questions of the interviewer or assignment editor ahead of time. As a public relations practitioner, this is a major part of your responsibilities. You must try to obtain details of the interview prior to having your client walk into the studio. A list of potential questions is the ultimate form of preparedness, while having a feel for the general direction and topics to be covered during the interview is the very least you can do for your client.

We have found that almost all broadcast outlets are willing to share many of the details of the interview ahead of time. After all, it's better for the interviewer to have a guest who appears to be learned rather than one who stumbles awkwardly throughout the interview. However, in order to protect the spontaneity of the interview, most hosts won't reveal all of the details prior to the interview. And in some instances, it is wise to provide the host with a list of prepared questions that your client is ready and willing to address.

Another major responsibility is to prepare your client as much as possible for any potentially dangerous or uncomfortable questions that may arise during the course of the interview. We find time and time again that you can never over prepare your client for a live TV or radio interview. There may be issues of confidentiality that need to be protected. Role playing with your client will ensure a preparedness that is essential for a successful television interview.

When speaking to a talk show host, it is advisable to have your client use the host's name during the interview. This subtle technique gives the interview a softer, more humanistic feel and sends a message to the audience that the person being interviewed is genuinely interested in what the host is asking of him or her.

Broadcast Options

As with the print media, there are many broadcast options that can be included as part of a national media relations campaign. For example, CNN offers the following programs, all of which rely in one way or another on public relations help to develop their shows: "Both Sides With Jesse Jackson," "Burden Of Proof," "Business Day," "The Capital Gang," "Early Edition," "Late Edition," "CNN Newsroom," "Perspectives," "Saturday Morning," "Sunday Morning," "Talkback Live," "Today," "World View," "Crossfire," "Earth Matters," "Global View," "Impact," "Inside Politics," "Larry King Live," "Managing with Lou Dobbs," "Moneyline," "Moneyweek," "Newsday," "Newsnight," "On The Menu," "Pinnacle," "Reliable Sources," "Science and Technology Week."

Each one of these shows should be examined for a possible match for your client. For example, "Pinnacle" presents a wonderful opportunity for public relations directors to pitch their CEOs to a show that highlights the life and career of top corporate executives. The program is always done in a tasteful, positive format and provides tremendous national and global exposure for the featured company and CEO.

National publicity comes in many shapes and sizes, and those public relations directors who are willing to invest some time and effort are likely to land influential broadcast interviews for their companies. The best way to begin any national media relations campaign is to research your options. Once you've narrowed your focus, you need to sit down and actually view the program that you want to pitch. For example, don't call the assignment editor at "The Road to the White House" on C-SPAN 2 without having prior knowledge of the show's format.

C-SPAN Opportunities

C-SPAN and C-SPAN 2 offer interesting possibilities for the PR consultant, and they have certainly played a very prominent role within our national media relations campaign for a number of years now. Based on North Capitol Street in downtown Washington, DC, many of C-SPAN's assignment editors and reporters are energetic and ambitious, and usually open to story ideas from PR people. The nice thing about C-SPAN is that they will often cover a live seminar or speech in its entirety, or tape the session and play back portions throughout their daily broadcasts. C-SPAN takes its responsibilities of providing the public with information about the government very seriously and will often cover events deemed too esoteric by the mainstream media.

The advent of C-SPAN and C-SPAN 2 has been a blessing for many institutions of higher learning and think tanks, whose research will often find its way onto the airwaves. We've learned that it can take a special kind of patience when working with C-SPAN on a story idea. For example, when the Annenberg Washington Program was about to release its findings on the shortage of organ donations due to a perceived lack of communications between the medical community and the public, we contacted C-SPAN and asked about the possibility of covering the event live.

The Annenberg Program decided to hold a half-day seminar on the topic that would include all kinds of experts in the field. At the same time, they would release the report. C-SPAN had worked with the Annenberg Program in the past and had always appreciated the cooperation and respect afforded them during the broadcast. They also liked the fact that the Annenberg Program was conveniently located in downtown Washington, and that its conference facilities were first rate and able to accommodate the voltage required by C-SPAN for all of their equipment.

We pitched the fact that the shortage of organ donors was becoming a national crisis, and that the seminar would outline ways to alleviate the problem. This was important to C-SPAN. They liked the fact that not only would a national problem be identified, but also possible solutions would be offered. After a lengthy, productive conversation with the assignment editor at C-SPAN, they all but assured us that they would cover the event live. They could not commit, however, due to the possibility of breaking news that day.

In order to accommodate C-SPAN, special arrangements needed to be made from a logistics standpoint, such as bringing in additional lighting, arranging the head table so that a wide angle shot could capture everyone involved, and getting permission from each of the speakers to have his or her speech broadcast.

We proceeded to do this, even though we knew that C-SPAN had backed out of other pre-scheduled events in the past – sometimes at the very last moment. Calls from us to the assignment editor the day before the seminar only added to our sense of frustration. C-SPAN said they would not know if they would cover the seminar until shortly before it began. They did indeed cover the event, and all the hard preparation was well worth the effort.

Allow me one more word about C-SPAN. It is more mobile than it used to be. Once focusing primarily on inside-the-beltway events, C-SPAN now goes all over the country to cover speeches, events, panel discussions and ceremonies.

You often can use print visibility to leverage broadcast visibility. The assignment editors and producers of national broadcast outlets religiously scan the wire services and major agenda-setting newspapers such as *The New York Times*, *The Wall Street Journal*, *Washington Post*, *Los Angeles Times* and *Christian Science Monitor* for story ideas. We have found over the years that one of the most effective avenues to broadcast visibility is to get major print visibility first. You can always send clips of newspaper and magazine stories to a producer as evidence that your story really is a story. Try it. You'll see that it works.

Chapter

Eight

Using Opinion Pieces and Letters to the Editor to Increase National Visibility

History of Op/eds

Once upon a time, not so long ago, the opinion editorial (op/ed) page in most newspapers was a relatively easy way to attain publicity for your CEO. You would meet briefly with your CEO to present him or her with the pre-conceived idea for a provocative, timely op/ed. The CEO would nod in approval and direct you to ghost write the piece. He or she might say, "Sounds good, but let me see it before you send it out."

After much research and time spent developing a solid lead, you had the piece the way you wanted it. The CEO gave it a quick once over and you were on your way. You double checked to make sure you had the CEO's name spelled correctly and title properly identified. After all, you couldn't afford to place "President" ahead of "CEO."

Depending on the size of your market, you either: 1) delivered the article to the city editor at the weekly newspaper (very small markets); 2) called the paper or scanned the masthead to discover the name of the editorial page editor and faxed the op/ed (medium sized market); 3) mailed the piece to the "Op/ed Editor" at a national newspaper.

If you were located in a small or medium market, the op/ed invariably appeared in print within a week or two. Your approving boss thought you were a hero. Perhaps you did this two or three times each year. Regardless of its contents, the piece never failed to be published. After all, the local newspaper was not about to anger such an upstanding citizen as your CEO, who just happened to be on the board of most of the local nonprofit groups. If you were brazen enough to try your luck with a national newspaper, you may have even been so fortunate as to have the op/ed published on occasion.

How things have changed. Today, the op/ed page has become a competitive hotbed with everyone throughout the public relations profession. What was once viewed as an afterthought is now considered prime territory for placements, so much so that entire seminars are devoted to the op/ed. For a hefty price, you can go hear a national op/ed editor tell you the dos and don'ts associated with writing and placing op/eds.

Let's begin by defining an op/ed. Simply stated, the op/ed is a cousin to the editorial. While the in-house editorial department of the newspaper writes the editorials, the op/ed is written and by-lined by an outside source. Sometimes the newspaper solicits this source, but usually the op/ed is sent in with no guarantee of being published. Both the editorial and op/ed are written from a point of view or opinion with a clear slant on a particular topic.

Op/ed is shorthand. It stands for "opposite editorial." It is named that not because it takes a viewpoint contrary to the newspaper's editorial policy, but because it traditionally appears on the right-hand page of the newspaper that is opposite the editorial page.

The odds these days of having your op/ed published are directly correlated to two factors: the strength of the piece and the circulation of the newspaper, with the latter being the most determining factor. Even the best of pieces will seldom find the light of day in such newspapers as *The New York Times, Wall Street Journal* and *Washington Post*. This is merely stating a fact and not meant to discourage you from trying, since placements in these news outlets do occur. Remember the odds, though; they are estimated at about one percent.

These odds increase directly proportionate to the name recognition of the author. It is the responsibility of every good public relations director to capitalize on the name recognition of a well-known CEO. For example, when we worked with Newton Minow of the Annenberg Washington Program, we took every available opportunity to push his name in front of an op/ed editor. The former Federal Communications Commissioner known for his "Vast Wasteland" speech of 1961 is surely a widely known commodity. His name alone as the author of an op/ed greatly increases its chances of being published. Evidently, op/ed editors believe that the more well known you are, the more interesting things you have to say.

Our very first recommendation to Mr. Minow, made to him no more than five minutes after meeting him for the first time, was to use his celebrity to increase the visibility of the Annenberg Washington Program (the non-profit he directed in the late 80s and early 90s.) His witty reply, "Even though my name appeared as an answer to a Jeopardy question, I'm not sure I'm that well-known. After all, it was a $500 question."

Nonetheless, Mr. Minow's name proved to be a valuable asset, as did his many insights and thoughts concerning telecommunications, and we helped develop and place numerous op/eds he authored in publications such as *The New York Times, Wall Street Journal, USA Today,* and the *Journal of Commerce.*

Perhaps the most important advice ever given to us concerning the writing of an op/ed came from Judy Dugan, assistant op/ed editor of *The Los Angeles Times.* "Don't spend too much time clearing your throat," she said. Translation: make your point quickly. Put your lead up front. Op/ed editors, like the public, are busy people with short attention spans who don't want to waste their time getting to the meaning of the editorial. If you don't capture their attention within the first paragraph, there's no chance of having your piece accepted for publication.

Opinion Piece Guidelines

In our experience, the op/eds with the best chances for success are those that address a timely, but not overworked, issue. Try to stay away from the same topics that George Will, Ellen Goodman and William Safire write about. If you cover the same ground as the syndicated columnists, the papers will use the syndicated writers and not your client. Your opinion piece must be thoughtful, stimulating, timely and provocative. Competition is fierce for the limited space that most newspapers reserve for these pieces.

Here are some guidelines for writing an opinion piece. You may stray somewhat from these, but the closer you come to this style the better your chances of being published. An effective opinion piece should:
- Focus on one idea and tell why it is important to readers
- Be timely
- Contain an element of controversy
- Come down clearly and strongly on one side of an issue (op/eds are meant to be opinions, that's the whole point)
- Be no more than 700 words, typewritten

- Be written for a general audience
- Avoid jargon or language that is too technical
- Make a point, and then back it up
- Put the lead (thesis) up front in the first 15 to 25 words – don't spend too much time clearing your throat.

Editors are looking for specific elements in an opinion piece. Make sure your op/ed contains the following:

- A variety of viewpoints
- A clearly identifiable voice: warm, witty, outraged, ironic, but never institutional
- Thoughtful, well-reasoned, well-researched pieces – not a series of assertions
- A real conclusion, sometimes a call for action or a position. Feel free to use the first-person voice
- A lead with your best punch (line) – tell readers what the article is about right off the bat so they know whether or not to continue reading
- Assertions that are backed up with facts. Op/eds lacking this are called "thumb suckers" and are not highly regarded by editors
- Viewpoints that are sustained throughout
- Tone that is informative, consistent, concerned, reasonable and responsible
- Information that they can get nowhere else; don't rehash what the nationally syndicated columnists are already saying.

Good writing skills will help your odds of getting published. Specific to op/ed pieces, your language and writing should:

- Be straightforward, vigorous, tight, and forceful
- Rely on strong verbs rather than adjectives or adverbs
- Avoid bulky leaden sentences
- Avoid clichés, mixed metaphors
- Avoid "which" clauses that make sentences too long, unwieldy
- Beware of tired little expressions that drag an editorial down – preachy phrases are not convincing
- Avoid complex sentences
- Use fresh, powerful images

- Pay attention to the words you normally use in making the argument; an editorial should sound as though a real person wrote it, and not a committee.

Ruby Scott's Submission Guidelines

When Ruby Scott oversaw the op/ed page of the *Chicago Tribune*, she judged submissions by the following criteria:

- Insightful commentary and opinion on the issues of the day
- Well-written essays, both weighty and whimsical
- Well-reasoned, expert analysis.

She would not accept:
- Ax grinding, spleen venting tirades
- Direct rebuttals of news stories or other op/ed articles; that's what the Letters to the Editors are for
- Self-serving advocacy pieces.

Ruby Scott has outlined some excellent guidelines for submitting your op/ed.

Articles should be 600 to 800 words, typed and double-spaced. All finished manuscripts (no drafts) must be accompanied by a cover letter containing your name, address, day and evening phones, Social Security number and credentials – i.e., your qualifications to write on the particular subject. You must have some expertise in the field or, in the case of an essay, some direct personal experience.

The volume of submissions is such that manuscripts cannot be returned nor their receipt acknowledged unless they are accompanied by a self-addressed stamped envelope.

The Chicago Tribune does not prefer and usually does not accept faxed submissions, however most major papers do. Almost all will not accept telephone queries. If your op/ed is accepted for publication, they will notify you before the article is published.

Multiple Submissions and Payments

Most major papers buy first rights only, which means you are free to submit your article to other publications after it has appeared in the Tribune. *The National Law Journal* currently is an example of a publication that retains all rights to a piece. Newspapers accepting op/eds fall into two categories: those that require exclusives and those that do not. An exclusive means that if the newspaper accepts the piece, no other newspaper can use it. There are grades of exclusivity, however.

If a paper accepts a piece on the basis of "all rights" that means the piece becomes its property and can be used for syndication. No other outlets have the rights to the piece. Many newspapers require exclusivity for "first rights." This means that after the newspaper publishes the piece, you are free to offer it elsewhere. Some outlets insist on regional exclusives. They don't want the piece offered simultaneously to other newspapers in the same or overlapping markets.

When Phil Joyce was op/ed editor of *The Philadelphia Inquirer*, for example, you would not offer a piece to *The Philadelphia Inquirer* and also to *The Allentown Morning Call*, only 40 miles away, since that would violate the *Inquirer's* requirement of regional exclusivity. Mr. Joyce didn't mind, however, if you offered the same piece to *The St. Louis Post-Dispatch* because it was a different media market.

Most major papers do not reprint articles that have appeared in other publications, but they understand that simultaneous submissions are sometimes necessary. So they ask you to notify them as soon as possible and withdraw your article if it has been accepted for publication elsewhere.

Op/eds are normally edited or trimmed as little as possible from the author's original submission, but op/ed editors do reserve the right to do so if necessary. From our experience, this is a painless procedure involving a little give and take on the part of the author or public relations representative. The meaning of the piece is not altered in any way. Usually, op/ed pieces are accepted or rejected "as they are."

And therein lies the beauty of the op/ed. A placement on the op/ed page is the only substantive way of having your views published without fear of words being taken out of context or being misconstrued in any way. Unlike an interview with a print or broadcast reporter, which most CEOs dread, op/eds afford the author the opportunity to carefully weigh his or her thoughts before putting them down on paper.

Many major newspapers, and some smaller ones, provide a nominal payment to the author of an op/ed, usually ranging from $50 to $200. This normally comes as a complete surprise to CEOs who write pieces solely for the purpose of getting their views seen by the public. One college president Dick Jones worked with appreciated the fact that the op/ed was written for him, and the president rewarded Mr. Jones with a briefcase he bought from his payment.

Placement Strategies

Although almost all op/ed editors say they don't like being called by the author of a piece or the public relations person representing the author, there are exceptions. You can develop a personal rapport with certain op/ed editors across the country by calling them prior to the submission of a piece to inquire if they are interested. This strategy is bolstered greatly if the piece happens to be written by someone well-known or by a widely recognized CEO, or if you have a good track record of placement with the targeted outlet.

National newspapers such as *The New York Times* and *The Wall Street Journal* and magazines such as *Newsweek* get so many inquiries about potential op/eds that they have established phone numbers for would-be authors and public relations people to call and learn submission guidelines, such as (1) how to submit a piece, (2) how many words it should contain and (3) how to check on its status. At this writing, both *The New York Times* and *The Wall Street Journal* have rejected your piece if you have not heard from the paper by the end of ten working days.

The following partial op/ed by Al Snyder, former director of the U.S. Information Agency and Fellow of the Annenberg Washington Program was published in no less than three major metropolitan newspapers.

Privatize Radio and TV Marti
By Al Snyder
Miami Herald, April 29, 1996

A State Department official recently provided to a gathering of diplomats, an over-view of U.S. foreign relations without once mentioning Cuba. Asked why Cuba had been omitted, the official replied that Cuba is no longer a foreign policy issue, it is a domestic political problem.

. . .The VOA, which enunciates U.S. ideals and foreign policies to audiences around the world, has always been uncomfortable supervising the politically oriented Cuba broadcasts. The VOA should have never been given oversight responsibility of a program service outside of its bailiwick. . . . Those best equipped to duke it out over the airwaves with Castro in his twilight years are Miami's Cuban Americans. The time has come for Washington to butt out.

Reprinted from the Miami Herald, © 1996. All rights reserved.

You will need to know the policies of the outlets to which you are submitting op/eds. If you accidentally break a taboo, it can taint your relationship with a newspaper.

In addition to the standard op/ed pages of newspapers, several major publications such as *The New York Times* and *Fortune Magazine* offer additional sections for specialized forums. For example, *The New York Times* at one point during the mid 1990s ran a Sunday Business Opinion section each week geared for the corporate reader. Seek out those special placement options.

The Manager's Journal column of *The Wall Street Journal* is another outlet for an outside commentary piece. Similar to an op/ed, this section deals with a very specific question or problem in management. The prospective author should provide as many real life examples as possible. Do not give armchair direction, but let the reader explore the question from specific case studies, rather from the author's personal opinion.

Whenever possible, specific characters and company names should be listed to give the article a real sense of credibility. Of course, this entails some added work for the author because of checks with the companies on details and, in some cases, permission. The only time when companies or people can be alluded to without specific name reference is when they represent a characterization that all readers will recognize from their own experience.

As an example of the best of the Manager's Journal, you can refer to "The Wall Street Journal on Management: The Best of the Manager's Journal," also available in paperback.

Scripps Howard News Service also offers a syndicated op/ed service, which gives authors the opportunity to have their opinions read by pockets of people throughout the entire country in those newspapers that subscribe to the service. It's a great way to reach those people who may not necessarily read *The New York Times* but who are loyal to their local papers.

Whenever we place an opinion piece on Scripps Howard News Service for one of our clients, it never fails that he or she hears from people in all parts of the nation. The difficult part about this type of placement is tracking the results. With *USA Today,* you have instant proof that the article ran. With Scripps Howard News Service, it's a different situation. You may receive a confirmation from its editor, but he can't tell you which papers ran the piece. Scripps Howard News Service makes selected op/eds available to its syndication base of more than 300 newspapers across the country.

Another wire service accepting op/eds is Bridge News, which provides news outlets with financial and economics information. You are fortunate if you can afford a clip service to track the results. If not, it's an arduous task to call selected papers or use the Internet to see if the piece ran in a certain paper. Even electronic searches such as Lexis-Nexis are not foolproof. Often papers load only their own work on such databases and neglect to upload wire service material.

Where can you find material for the op/ed page? Annual reports often serve as fodder for provocative, timely pieces. Speeches by CEOs are another good source. The best way, however, to develop an op/ed is to sit down with your CEO and pick his or her brain. Pretend you're a reporter and ask leading, open-ended questions in order to gather the information needed to write the op/ed.

Don't get discouraged if your initial attempts at the national op/ed pages fail to produce any published essays. Broaden your focus and include newspapers such as the *Atlanta Journal Constitution, Baltimore Sun, Dallas Morning News,* or the *Seattle Post.* These publications may not be *The New York Times,* but they are very respected news outlets nonetheless. We have frequently targeted the *Christian Science Monitor* as our choice for many of the op/eds we develop. And even though the *Monitor* is not among the nation's largest papers, its op/ed page is widely regarded and respected as an excellent source of commentary. Among its regular readers are the most influential leaders in the world.

Another strategy to keep in mind when trying to place an op/ed is to clearly identify the audience you're trying to reach. For example, if the piece is about telecommunications and it has been rejected by all of the first tier publications, you might aim for the *Atlanta Journal Constitution* since that city is fast becoming the hot bed for communications companies. Likewise, an essay about computers could be sent to the *Seattle Post.*

We used the op/ed page as part of a national media plan for Marywood University and concentrated on the issue of Catholic identity; Marywood has enjoyed a long tradition as a Catholic institution. This information was included in an op/ed by our president entitled, "Can Catholic Schools Keep Their Religious Identity in the 1990s?" It received play in a number of major metropolitan newspapers along with some very prominent educational journals.

You can help augment a news story with an op/ed page. For example, if you are trying to package a news story on a decrease in tuition (a rare occurrence) at a college or university, you'll probably want to include - in addition to pitch letters and media sessions - an op/ed by the president detailing the reasons behind such a bold decision and the strategies that will make it work.

You can often parley op/ed placements into talk show appearances by sending a tear sheet to assignment editors at radio and television stations. When a sociologist at the University of California Berkeley began to have his op/eds published in national newspapers, not coincidentally did his phone begin ringing from national television and radio talk show hosts who needed to book a certain number of guests each week.

Let's say all your efforts fail and no one accepts the piece. This seems to be happening more frequently of late due to the sheer number of op/eds being written these days. Never fear. Your efforts may not be in vain. A well-developed op/ed can usually find a home in the local newspaper or the company newsletter, thus bringing a sense of pride to those connected with the company. Also, developing an op/ed is always an excellent way to discover the pertinent issues that are affecting the company or nonprofit, and it can lead to the development of news releases or pitches to national media outlets.

The following op/ed was altered slightly and placed in three distinct news outlets.

An Impartial Jury, Not an Ignorant One
Op/Ed Piece
By Newton N. Minow, Director, Annenberg Washington Program
Wall Street Journal, June 5, 1990

Jury selection in the drug and perjury trial of Washington Mayor Marion Barry began yesterday. Can Mayor Barry get a fair trial in Washington in the face of intensive pre-trial publicity? Yes, as long as the court fulfills its constitutional duty to empanel an impartial, not ignorant, jury.

The Sixth Amendment to the Constitution requires that criminal defendants be tried by an "impartial jury of the State and district wherein the crime shall have been committed." Many judges, however, equate "impartial" with uninformed.

The problem is not a new one. In 1871, Mark Twain described the system by which jurors are selected as putting "a ban upon intelligence and honesty, and a premium upon ignorance, stupidity, and perjury." Twain's concern was that judges were responding to the dramatic expansion of the media – in 1871, "telegraph and newspapers" – by banning informed citizens from juries.

Today technology, combined with an insatiable public curiosity, has led to an explosion in news coverage and dramatic reenactments of crimes. The average hours of TV usage by household is 7.2 hours a day: average radio usage is almost three hours a day. And more than 64% of American households read newspapers. It is next to impossible for a citizen to be unaware of major crimes in his community. Even on the national level, Manueal Noriega, Lt. Col. Oliver North, Exxon Valdez tanker captain Joseph Hazelwood, billionaire Leona Helmsley, as well as Mayor Barry, are household names.

Some judges dismiss potential jurors merely because they are media-literate. Other judges, concerned about the possibility of not being able to seat a jury in media-intensive trials, go the opposite way and – running roughshod over the Sixth Amendment – ignore suggestions of deep bias from potential jurors. The apparent majority, however, take a middle road and attempt to inquire about possibly biasing media exposure and to determine whether that exposure will affect the ability of jurors to be impartial.

The primary means through which they do this is voir dire. Through a series of questions, the judge (and/or, in many courts, attorneys) questions potential jurors in an effort to determine whether they can be impartial. Many critics argue that voir dire fails to elicit accurate or honest responses from potential jurors. Who is going to admit publicly to being a bigot? In fact, some attorneys believe that potential jurors admit prejudice only as a convenient means of avoiding jury duty.

Many jurors underestimate their exposure, but with follow-up questions demonstrate considerable knowledge about the case. For instance, in the State v. Copeland trail, in which a black defendant was tried in Medart, Fla., for the brutal 1978 murder of a 19-year-old white woman, one juror denied having any knowledge of the case, but admitted upon further questioning to having "read about it in the newspaper and even discussed it."

Even when the voir dire is conducted in the judge's chambers away from the public and press scrutiny, the procedure is rife with impediments to identifying jurors most likely to be impartial. For instance, judges and lawyers often indicate the answers they want. In Copeland the judge asked: "You haven't read about it (the case) or heard it on television or anything or discussed it with anybody whereby you might have formed an opinion about the case?" And, "well, from what you're telling me, then, you could sit here and be fair and impartial and listen to the evidence as it comes to you, as it is presented in this courtroom and based solely on that evidence?" Effective voir dire questions are difficult to frame. Vague, open-ended queries frequently fail to elicit information about possible bias. Jurors may not understand what information is prejudicial or improper, or may not even be aware that they have been exposed to prejudicial publicity. Specific questions, on the other hand, may give the potential juror exactly the information the attorney wants to be certain the juror does not have.

But the ineffectiveness of existing techniques for identifying and minimizing the impact of bias does not mean that Mayor Barry cannot get a fair trial. The key lies in defining an impartial juror. Jurors are not value free and juries are not blank slates. Nor were they intended to be.

The Supreme Court has identified a number of essential roles for juries. The most important, according to the court, is to protect citizens against "arbitrary law enforcement," "the corrupt or overzealous prosecutor," and "the compliant, biased, or eccentric judge."

Juries, the court has written, "interpose between the accused and his accuser the common-sense judgment of a group of laymen." If it is to safeguard liberty, protect against official malfeasance and represent the community – as well as determine the guilt or innocence of the accused – the jury must be composed of members with diverse backgrounds, experience and views. This is why cases are decided by juries and not individual jurors. The jurors should also be active, informed members of the community. In fact, the skills of discernment that most citizens exercise and refine daily in evaluating the barrage of news, advertising and rhetoric presented by the media may help jurors to be both impartial and capable. As the Supreme Court wrote almost 30 years ago, "It is sufficient if the juror can lay aside his impression or opinion and render a verdict based on the evidence presented in court."

The role of courts, then, is not to eliminate all potential jurors who are media literate, ignore all evidence of possible media induced bias, or rely blindly on ineffective, ill-targeted methods for controlling bias. Rather, courts must inquire specifically as to what each potential juror knows about the case, whether he holds opinions about the guilt or innocence of the defendant, and whether those opinions can be laid aside and a verdict rendered based on the facts admitted into evidence.

This will help the court judge potential jurors' credibility and the likelihood they can render a decision based on the evidence. Perhaps more important, it will help potential jurors consider their own ability to live up to the constitutional requirement of impartiality and help them guard against improper bias throughout the trial.

As Mark Twain said: "In this age, when a gentleman of high social standing, intelligence, and probity swears that testimony given under solemn oath will outweigh, with him, street talk and newspaper reports based upon mere hearsay, he is worth a hundred jurymen who will swear to their own ignorance and stupidity, and justice would be far safer in his hands than in theirs. Why could not the jury law be so altered as to give men of brains and honesty an equal chance with fools and miscreants?"

Reprinted from The Wall Street Journal © 1990 Dow Jones & Company, Inc. All rights reserved.

There are a few interesting and salient points that should be made concerning this op/ed by Newton Minow. First, it reads over 1,100 words, which surpasses the normally accepted word count of 700 words by quite a bit. Once again, we refer to the author. Someone like Newton Minow, Henry Kissinger or Jimmy Carter can break the rules and get away with it because of the name recognition. Other not-so-famous authors should try and adhere to the 700-word limit in order to increase their placement chances.

Also, when you examine the Minow op/ed, you quickly see that it follows the format presented earlier in this chapter. Mr. Minow makes his point quickly and focuses on one idea – that impartial juries can be seated despite intense pre-trial publicity. He uses a warm, witty voice throughout and the piece is well researched and timely. His assertions (that impartial juries are possible) are backed up by his references to the findings of the Supreme Court and to the critique of present voir dire techniques.

His use of strong verbs such as "safeguards, demonstrate, eliminate, fulfills," is evident throughout the piece. Keep in mind that a strong verb does not equate to the length of the word, an unusual meaning, or one that's hard to pronounce. Strong verbs are active rather than passive. Above all, Mr. Minow cleverly uses Mark Twain to make his conclusion that even high profile defendants can indeed receive a fair and impartial trial if certain procedures are followed.

Letters To The Editor

Letters to the Editor are a very good – and often overlooked – way to attain national publicity for your organization or corporation.

Unlike the opinion piece (op/ed), a letter to the editor is almost always a direct result of an article that was previously published by a newspaper or magazine. In many cases, it is a rebuttal of the reporter's views expressed throughout the published article. However, it can also support those views.

Since letters to the editor refute or support a published article, op/ed, editorial, or another letter to the editor, timing is everything. It is imperative that you formulate and send in your letter to the editor within a day or two after the article you are referring to was published. Like any other aspect of national publications, the space is very limited and the competition is fierce. Although you may think your view is unique, each major newspaper receives hundreds of letters to the editor each day from readers referring to the same article. Only the timely, provocative letters get published.

Letters to the Editor Guidelines

Letters to the Editor should respond to something that appeared in the newspaper or magazine, preferably an article that was written by one of the publication's staffers. Most publications feel a responsibility to offer comment from readers, particularly if it is tied directly to an article that was printed in the publication.

Here are some guidelines for writing letters to the editor:

- Keep them short. Letters in the major weekly news magazines are often only a sentence in length. *The New York Times* will on occasion run letters several paragraphs long. In general, however, the bigger the publication, the shorter the letter should be.
- Make one point. Resist the temptation to correct three mistakes in the article you're commenting on. Pick the most important issue and address that.
- Do it now. Don't wait to write letters to the editor. Major publications do not print every letter they get. They use a representative sample. If yours gets there early you stand a better chance. E-mail or fax in your letter.
- Credit your organization. Make sure your company's name gets used. If the letter is from the president, sign it "John Smith, President, XYZ Corporation."

The following letter to the editor is a fine example of following the guidelines.

**Letter to the Editor
Free to Speak, but Willing to Listen and Learn
New York Times, April 17, 1990**

In "Why Tolerate Campus Bigots?" (Op-Ed, April 6), James Laney, president of Emory University, makes the case for banning "discriminatory harassment." Such measures are ultimately counter-productive and doomed to failure. The First Amendment encourages robust debate, and the Supreme Court allows for few restrictions in its exercise. The "fighting words" exception to free speech guarantees cannot be expanded to meet the challenges of uncivil campus words and behavior.

We have just completed a symposium on this topic at the Marshall Wythe School of Law at the College of William and Mary, and the speakers, all eminent legal scholars, debated the legitimacy of university regulations to protect against hate speech.

After careful discussion, a large audience of students and community members overwhelmingly rejected such techniques to regulate civility on campus. The difficulty is that such regulations are incapable of even-handed application. It is almost impossible to define precisely the types of speech that quality for regulation as discriminatory harassment. At one extreme is conduct involving discrimination or harassment – the types of overt misconduct prohibited under such laws as the Civil Rights Act of 1964. No one doubts that universities, like all other American institutions, can and must police such discriminatory behavior.

At the other extreme are expressions of opinion espousing repugnant theories of racial or sexual superiority – intellectual propositions that virtually all reject, but that cannot be censored if we are to embrace freedom of speech as an academic value of transcendent importance. Unfortunately, most of the racist and sexist attacks that proponents of new campus controls wish to sanction do not fall into these extremes, but into a vast middle area where speech, conduct, opinion and emotion and intertwined.

Ultimately, campuses must rely on noncoercive techniques to deal with nasty, rude and uncivil behavior. Expressions of concern by such university leaders as Mr. Laney are critical to creating an atmosphere where civility is respected. But that state – which is not always compatible with learning and growth – cannot be established by administrative decree.

The greater challenge for us is to create an environment where all are free to speak, but by common accord each is also willing to listen and learn. Community standards can achieve voluntary accords without jeopardizing the values of academic freedom behind the First Amendment, which must at all events be respected by the academy.

PAUL R. VERKUIL
President, College of William and Mary

Chapter
Nine

Damage Control in High Profile Situations

There are times throughout one's career in the public relations field that you will be asked to put out a fire or, at the very least, you'll be asked to stop a small fire from spreading beyond control. When this happens, you need to know the methodology and philosophy behind damage control.

There have been many high-profile, well-documented situations over the past several years that have resulted in some very negative press for those involved. Of course, the Exxon Valdez oil spill immediately comes to mind. Those of us in the wordsmith business had to cringe as mistake followed mistake in the form of media relations. "Deny all wrongdoing," seemed to be Exxon's mantra at the outset of the disaster. Or worse yet, their public relations people evidently thought that if they ignored the problem it would eventually go away.

Their handling of the incident proved to be textbook in terms of what not to do following a negative situation. In fact, the public relations strategy will live in infamy in the annals of Public Relations 101. Sadly enough, however, is the fact that many other high profile individuals and companies failed to learn from Exxon Valdez.

We are now all familiar with another classic example of failing to accept responsibility for one's own actions. "I did not have sex with that woman!" The price to be paid in this case: impeachment proceedings.

There's no doubt that lying or running from the truth can damage a reputation in ways that may never be repaired. And surely the "ostrich in the sand" approach has never been shown to be an effective public relations strategy. Denial is even worse. Just ask Richard Nixon. Sometimes it takes a long time – even years – but the truth does come out.

On the other hand, coming clean appears to be able to help salvage not only the image of an individual or company, but their public worth as well. Dick Morris, the one-time advisor to President Clinton, knows this as well as anyone. After his infamous infidelity scandal threatened to jolt him into obscurity, he quickly took the blame for his actions and asked forgiveness from the public via the talk show circuit. In fact, he seemed to be on all of the national talk shows each time you turned on the television. He knew the value of national exposure far better than most. All was well again with the public and he has since resurfaced time and time again as a talking head on one network after the other. Ours is a nation ready – and seemingly even eager – to forgive transgressions. We believe in second chances. The one we are unprepared to forgive is the one who tries to cover up mistakes.

Be as forthright and timely as possible with information concerning negative circumstances within your organization. This is not to say that you have to divulge everything. Neither the press nor the public needs every small detail of a scandal or controversial issue. There are limitations on what needs to be said, and it's the responsibility of public relations departments to be able to distinguish between these fine lines of reasoning. Legalities may sometimes play a role in how you respond to the media's request for specific information.

If you work as the communications director for a health care system, you need to know the code of conduct dictated by the Patient's Bill of Rights Act. This Act dictates the limited information that can be released to the media regarding the status of a patient. If your hospital happens to have a high profile patient, the media's interest for information is often insatiable. You're likely to be paged at all hours by people wanting to know if there have been any changes on the status of the patient. You are obligated to reply, but only with the condition of the patient. Be prepared, because the media will be insistent. "Is his family holding a vigil by his side 24 hours a day?" "What's his prognosis?"

Remain firm and answer with the medical condition only. However, in order to maintain your good relationship with the media, promise them that you have developed a "call" list of reporters who will be contacted at the fist sign of any change in the condition of the patient. It is prudent to have a wire service, such as Associated Press, at the top of this "call" list. That way, you will be assured that all media outlets will be informed of any changes through the wire service. Similarly, in higher education, you need to know about the Buckley Amendment, which limits the amount of information colleges can release about their students. Are you doing business on-line? You can be sure that your use of customer information will come under increasing scrutiny, especially if you market to children.

Being proactive certainly can help a company or institution in time of crisis. Case in point: the University of Louisville was under tremendous pressure for accepting a bid to the Fiesta Bowl football game in Phoenix, Arizona, in 1990. At the time, the entire country was loquaciously condemning the bowl game for a perceived discrimination against blacks. How could the University of Louisville, with its African American football players, participate in such an event?

We quickly advised Donald Swain, then president of the University of Louisville, to gather all the facts behind the decision to participate in the bowl game and make them public. We suggested an op/ed. Because you have control over what is being said in an op/ed, it seemed only logical to try this approach first. We also believed that the op/ed should come from the top, Mr. Swain himself, and not the football coach or athletic director.

Time was of the essence since the criticism of the university gathered more and more momentum each day through the media and various civic groups. We met with President Swain and the university's public relations director, Denise Fitzpatrick, to brainstorm the direction the op/ed would take. We all agreed it had to be an honest assessment of the overall situation, but unapologetic in tone. On the contrary, the piece needed to be forceful and carefully crafted in order to explain the university's decision.

As soon as our meeting ended, we called the sports department of *The New York Times* and spoke to the editor in charge of the sports page's op/ed (*The New York Times* was one of the few papers to have had such a section in its Sunday edition). He agreed that the topic was of national interest and, without making any promises, he encouraged the University of Louisville to submit the op/ed. It was published the following Sunday.

Why Louisville Accepted the Fiesta Bowl Bid
By Donald Swain
President, University of Louisville
New York Times, November 18, 1990

. . .Let there be no mistake about our reasons. We are going to
Phoenix not only because our football team will be able to participate at a higher level of competition and recognition in athletics, but
also because it will give us an opportunity to honor the legacy of
Dr. Martin Luther King, Jr.

The university has been observing King's birthday since 1984. We
favor affirmative action, diversity and civil rights, and we support
the values advocated by King. . . .

Some critics have accused us of emphasizing money over morality
in making our decision, citing the $2.5 million we could receive in
bowl revenue. Yet we are hoping to use a substantial portion of that
money to advance the very causes King stood for.

. . .In the midst of the political rhetoric surrounding the decision, I
urge everybody to remember that this is a football game. Our football team is 9-1-1 this season. The players – black, brown and
white – vote unanimously to play. This fact weighed heavily in our
final decision. Had they said they preferred to stay away, the university would have not accepted the bowl bid.

Is it morally wrong for young men who have worked hard to
achieve lofty athletic goals to see them finally realized? Would it be
more ethical if these collegiate football players, who had no say in
the Arizona political process, passed on the opportunity of a life-
time? I don't think so.

As the Cardinal wide receiver Anthony Cummings stated succinctly:
"Dr. King had a dream. I have one too. This is my dream. He was
the one who fought so we could play football."

Excerpt of original article. Reprinted from The New York Times, ©
1990. All rights reserved.

In addition to the op/ed, we arranged interviews for President Swain with several national radio programs. During each, he calmly outlined the reasons behind the decision but remained steadfast in his premise that it was a good decision. Of course, there will be times when you must admit to a mistake or gross error in judgment. If that's the case, so be it. Do it and move on with your business.

Another decisive way to combat a crisis situation is to hold a news conference, acknowledge the problem, and offer recommendations to help alleviate the situation.

Don't rely on someone from the public relations office sending out press releases filled with corporate propaganda. The crisis management strategies need to include the president and/or CEO.

There are many mistakes companies or individuals make when trying to right a wrong: trying to justify the error by rambling babble; taking too long to respond; ignoring the problem and hoping it will go away. But the one mistake that will always come back to haunt you is not being honest with your response. The public is very forgiving if you give them the chance. If Pete Rose had heeded this advice, his #14 would almost assuredly be sitting proudly in Cooperstown this day.

Knight Ridder newspapers ran an article at the end of the millennium concerning the biggest public relations disasters of 1999. According to a list compiled by Fineman Associates, a San Francisco public relations firm, the disasters include blunders by some real heavyweights in the corporate sector, along with some well-known individuals. Fineman Associates cited duplicity, myopia, paranoia, sloth and overkill as cardinal sins when dealing with the public.

The public relations firm says Microsoft was guilty of rushing to put a positive spin on each day's events during its antitrust lawsuit with the government, and "niggling over the meaning of e-mails in court." The software giant also won PR demerits for financially backing a think tank whose newspaper ads supported Microsoft's position. "Such obvious duplicity is damaging to Microsoft, and it's damaging to public relations," said *Inside PR Newsletter*.

Also on the list were the major league baseball umpires. When 57 of the 68 umpires decided to quit to force contract concessions, they may not have guessed that baseball owners would call their bluff. But owners began hiring new umps and the public didn't rally to support the former umps' cause.

The Rev. Jerry Falwell took a public relations beating, according to Fineman. Falwell's newspaper, the *National Liberty Journal*, invited public scorn when it claimed that one of the Teletubbies, Tinky Winky, was a gay role model. The rationale: the character's purple color and red purse are gay symbols. "The press was depicting Falwell as a paranoid, sexually obsessed holy roller," reported Fineman.

The top management of *The Los Angeles Times* was also cited for using poor judgment when they devoted a Sunday magazine section to the new Staples Arena and didn't tell reporters or readers it was sharing the advertising revenue with the arena.

Also making the list was the Exxon Corporation. The company lobbied and sued to allow the Exxon Valdez, which ten years previously spilled millions of gallons of oil into Prince William Sound, to return to its original Alaska-California route. The tanker had been banned from returning to the Sound.

Coca-Cola Company in Belgium and France was added to the list when 200 people got sick after drinking Coke. Ten days into the crisis, CEO Douglas Ivester flew to Brussels and apologized for the problem. His failure to react quickly may have turned Coca-Cola into "the poster child of ghastly crisis management and bad PR," according to *PR Week* columnist Frank Mankiewicz. Ivester resigned soon after.

Finally, there's the case of the American Medical Association. Dr. George Lundberg, editor of the Journal of the American Medical Association, was dismissed after publishing an article on college students' views that oral sex didn't fit their definition of sex. News reports hinted that the AMA was influenced by politics after the President Clinton scandal.

In at least some of these examples, the worst of the crisis could have been avoided if the CEO or company spokesperson reacted quickly and honestly. Trying to put a false positive spin on a negative story or crisis will only add fuel to the fire and can damage your reputation beyond repair.

Bill Gates, Chairman and CEO of Microsoft, made several sound PR decisions after the court ruled against Microsoft during round one of the federal antitrust lawsuit. All of a sudden, Bill Gates the enigma became Bill Gates the human being by appearing on a variety of national talk shows. During each interview, Mr. Gates appeared relaxed and confident. He did not attack his accusers, but underscored all of the positive reasons why Microsoft has become the dominant player within the software industry. The question remains: Was Gates' positive PR move in time to restore its lofty image?

Another relevant example of damage control was the attempt by Philip Morris Corporation to unleash a new public image after years of both legal and public relations setbacks concerning the harmfulness of tobacco. Jennifer Mann of Knight Ridder reported that Steven C. Parrish, a Philip Morris senior vice president, crisscrossed the land telling the public how the company that purveys tobacco and alcohol also sells food products and is doing its part to help Americans. It's a dramatic change, reports Mann, from the company's previous communications strategies with regard to the public and the media.

She reported: "For so long, we've been perceived as being bad and only about tobacco," said Parrish. "And a lot of that was our fault. The media would call and all they got was a 'no comment.' They had no idea of what we were doing for the community, if anything."

This illustrates an important point. You can't expect to get a fair shake from the media if all you're doing is hiding from them or offering "no comment" in times of crisis. You need to be proactive and forthright, perhaps take your lumps and move on to the positive aspects within your company or institution.

We also tell each of our clients that national media relations is a two-way street, and if you expect to have them listen to your pitches about positive story ideas, then you must be willing to talk with them during times of trouble. It's the only way you can establish the credibility necessary to ensure desired results at the national level.

Conclusion

By now you're either excited about the possibility of beginning your own national media relations campaign, or you've decided you have neither the time or available resources necessary to implement such a large-scale project.

We hope you'll take the plunge and move forward with plans to attain national visibility for your organization. Like most things worthwhile, you can't expect desired results unless you're prepared to commit the energy associated with a national media relations campaign. Even if you opt to use a consultant, you need to be a second set of hands to assist with the intricate details involved with seeking national publicity.

For example, you need to identify those story ideas that you believe warrant national media attention. A consultant cannot be expected to come to campus or corporate headquarters and know those story ideas worth pursuing without your guidance. You know your organization and you should have some sense of where the national features will come from.

The amount of time you are willing to devote to the national media consultant will directly determine the success or failure of your national media relations campaign. If you can only talk or meet with your consultant on an inconsistent basis, expect inconsistent results. There's no doubt that the best results we ever garner for our clients stem from a mutual respect between the public relations director and us. We try not to intrude on one another's role. We view the public relations directors we work with as invaluable to the process, and without them nothing substantive could be accomplished. They understand their organization and the people who work there. In return, we understand the national media.

And learning to play by the rules of the game also will help. For example, always adhere to the deadlines set forth by a national reporter who may have contacted you as the result of a pitch letter. If he or she needs quotes from one of your expert employees or CEO by 5 p.m., get them to the reporter by 4 p.m. This often means conveying the importance of the request to the expert in honest terms.

Can you achieve big time recognition for your organization without the assistance of a national media relations consultant? Absolutely. However, be prepared to delegate some of your normal responsibilities to others within your department. You'll need to free up some time.

Let's re-emphasize some of the points made throughout the book.

- Always confirm media sessions with national reporters the day before the visit. Nothing equals the value of arranging face-to-face meetings with reporters in New York, Washington, D.C. or Los Angeles in order to discuss a potential story idea. It's the best way we know to introduce a story idea to a national reporter. But even the best intentions sometimes go awry. Breaking news, an emergency, or simply a forgetful reporter can result in the cancellation of a media session, especially if you forgot to confirm the session the day before. Do yourself a favor. Call the reporter(s) and leave a message indicating the date and time of the scheduled meeting.

- Don't rely on media guides. Call the media outlet and confirm reporters. Although media guides are important tools of the trade, they are not foolproof. When contacting national reporters, you need to have accurate names, or all the time and energy you've invested to this point in identifying stories will be wasted. It's highly unlikely the appropriate reporter will ever receive your pitch letter or phone call if that reporter isn't correctly identified at the onset.

- Include national trade publications as part of your national media relations plan. No one director who embarks on a national media relations plan should expect to score exclusively with the mainstream national media. It simply won't happen. Do yourself a favor and also pitch story ideas to the many trade publications that are part of the publishing world. First of all, the odds of landing a placement in *Modern Healthcare* are much greater than in *Time*. Moreover, having the name of your organization in *Industry Week* surely beats the heck out of seeing it appear in the *Siwash Gazette*, your local hometown newspaper. And once the story runs, clip it and include it in your annual report. Send tear sheets to Board members. They love knowing they are a part of an organization worthy of high-powered attention.

- Whenever possible, use op/eds as part of your national media relations plan. Nothing warms the heart more than seeing the name of your CEO or one of your experts appear next to an op/ed in *The Wall Street Journal*. First of all, the piece runs virtually unedited. Secondly, it appears in one of the most widely read sections of the newspaper. And although the odds of placing a national op/ed are becoming increasingly difficult, success will come if the subject is right. When success does come your way, it's like the "shot heard round the world." Peers from across the country will take notice, because most of them will either see the piece or hear about it.

- Provocative pitch letters are essential when trying to attain national publicity. If there's one thing that will capture the attention of a national reporter, it's a well-conceived, well-crafted pitch letter. Think of pitch letters as your first impression. If you make a good impression, your chances of receiving callbacks are greatly increased. Some of the world's best story ideas have surely gone unreported due to an inadequate pitch letter. Above all, be concise and accurate with your information. Leave contact phone numbers for both you and for the person you're hoping will be interviewed. If possible, include day and night time phone numbers, e-mail addresses and fax numbers. Tell the reporter what time of day is best to reach you. Make it very easy for reporters should they decide to call you back. Also, keep your pitch letters to one page.

- Not all story ideas are meant for national news outlets. This is sometimes a tough call because your expert, president, or CEO may be insisting that their story has national potential written all over it. As the media relations expert, you need to make a decision on the story's potential and stand firm with that decision. Don't promise a placement in *USA Today* if the story is better suited for *The Chronicle of Higher Education*. And even then, don't make promises at all. Although the trade journals may present a better opportunity for placement, there is never a guarantee that your story will see the light of day. It's best to emphasize this important fact up front with the person who is the subject of the pitch. Tell her you believe this story has great potential, and share with her your plans to market it. But never promise that a reporter will be calling for quotes.

- C-SPAN offers great potential for features, and if you are in higher education, don't forget them. Perhaps C-SPAN believes they conventionally reach an erudite audience, thus the wide array of educational forums that appear on their broadcasts. Whatever the reason, there's no denying the educational bent to which C-SPAN espouses. If you work for a college or university and wish to implement a national media relations campaign, you should be on the lookout for seminars that may appeal to C-SPAN. Well-known speakers will help attract C-SPAN to your location, as do national trends and unique events. Be sure and notify C-SPAN well in advance of the pending event.

- Limit your phone conversation to 60 seconds with a national reporter. Don't sit there with a stopwatch, of course, but be aware that national reporters are very busy people with limited time for phone calls. You'll find that you'll be able to steal several minutes of their precious time once you begin to establish a professional rapport with them. But this may not happen with your first contact. It takes time to establish and nurture your relationship. Credibility is the key here. If reporters know you've been a good source for story ideas in the past, they'll be more inclined to give you more time to make your pitch. Both Dick and I have developed numerous contacts over the years with national reporters whom we've come to know on personal level through phone calls and media sessions. When we call these people, we're pretty confident they won't cut us off before we have the chance to make our pitch. They know we only call when we have something they may be interested in, and we also know enough to respect their time limitations. They want to hear a friendly "hello" followed quickly by the story idea. More often than not, they'll politely refuse to delve further into the issue and will indicate they don't intend to follow up on your story idea. It's the nature of the business we're in. Be prepared to accept this right of refusal. Being persistent is one thing. Being pig-headed is another. Know when to thank the reporter for his time and move on to another media outlet. Just because *The Los Angeles Times* isn't enthralled with your story on cloning cabbages, that's no reason not to pitch it to National Public Radio.

• National news reporters don't necessarily care where the story idea came from as long as it's a good story. Sure, the University of California Berkeley will have more national story ideas than Marywood University. But Marywood University, like any other college or university, will have its fair share. And your small company will certainly have a story or two that has national potential. Just keep looking. You'll find them. When you do, don't succumb to an inferiority complex because you don't represent one of the Ivies or a Fortune 500 Company. Have confidence in your ability to discover a good news story based on substance alone and convey that confidence either in your voice as you pitch the concept to a national reporter or in the tone of your pitch letter.

- When traveling to New York or Washington, DC, always try to book at least four media sessions. Is it worth the trip to New York City for one media session, even if that session happens to be with *The New York Times?* Well, that probably depends on your point of origin. If you are located in northeastern Pennsylvania or New Jersey, the answer is definitely "yes." A 90-minute or two-hour drive is no problem in order to meet with *The New York Times.* However, even in this scenario it's always prudent to try and book a few other meetings with national reporters. Use discretion and do not arrange media sessions with competitive media in case one of the reporters happens to like the story idea. You don't want to be in the embarrassing position of having to cancel your next appointment with the business reporter at *The Wall Street Journal* should *The New York Times* appear likely to do the story. A good mix of media sessions for the day would be a major newspaper reporter, a respected trade journal, a national magazine and a national network. This may seem like a difficult goal, but it's worth the time and effort even if you fall short. And you may succeed in attaining commitments from two or three of these media outlets. Cultivating your relationships with reporters is an important long-term goal. Maybe they won't book your expert the first time, but your next story may appeal to them.

- Judy Dugan of the editorial pages at *The Los Angeles Times* has some wise advice: Don't spend too much time "clearing your throat" in an op/ed. It's hard enough trying to place an op/ed that's very well done. If your lead isn't clear immediately, your piece won't stand of chance of being published. Spend as much time crafting a good lead as you would with the entire piece. Rewrite it until you're completely satisfied with its message.

- Always develop "crib" sheets before phoning a national reporter. Since you have precious little time to convey your pitch to a national reporter, jotting down the important facts you need may save time during the conversation. You may be nervous calling national reporters and they may ask difficult questions of you. With crib sheets, you have a security blanket of sorts. Don't write a narrative. Instead, formulate a few bullet points. You'll find that such a practice may alleviate some of your anxiety.

- Scan the national newspapers every day. Only by keeping abreast of reporters' responsibilities can you be sure you're pitching a story idea to the appropriate person. Media guides can be helpful, but don't rely on them exclusively. Reporters change beats and you need to know this. Also pay attention to the credits at the end of network television shows to discover names of assignment editors or bookers. By knowing the names of the national reporters, you'll increase your odds of connecting with one of them for a possible placement.

- Whenever possible, include the president or CEO of an organization in your national media relations plan. The importance of this strategy cannot be overstated for several reasons. First, you need your president's support in order to devote the time and money needed to implement a national media relations campaign. You need to have your president talk up the concept with key members of the organization you represent. If key employees know that the president supports the idea of national publicity, it's far easier to ask their cooperation in relaying interesting story ideas to you. And when the national media happen to call (in all likelihood after receiving a pitch letter from you,) asking cooperation of those key employees becomes easier. Also, many national issues require the attention of a president or CEO and reporters like the idea that they can talk to the person in charge.

- Look for national news ideas in trends or traditions. Does your college have a tradition in which the president serves lunch to the students? Or do faculty members dress up like characters from a play by Shakespeare and take their courses to the local elemen-

tary schools? Do all of your corporate executives volunteer a
week of their time each year to build houses for Habitat For
Humanity? Has your secretarial pool displayed the uncanny ability to have correctly picked the last seven presidential elections?
If so, you may be sitting on a national news story. Look at all possible story ideas when national trends occur.

- Always include a wire service in your national media relations
  plan. Often taken for granted, wire services offer a grand way to
  achieve big time recognition. Perhaps nothing, not even a placement on CNN, equals the exposure of having The Associated
  Press or Scripps Howard News Service run one of your story
  ideas. Keep in mind that wire services serve newspapers throughout virtually all pockets of the country, and people who don't
  necessarily get the opportunity to read the major newspapers will
  see a placement about your organization via the wire services.

- Once you have a national clip, run with it. Use it in annual
  reports and in-house publications. Include it in ad campaigns, if
  practical. Don't assume that all of your key constituents read *The
  Washington Post* or listen to National Public Radio. In fact, most
  don't. It's great that over one million readers may have seen your
  placement in *USA Today*, but you want to be sure that all of
  your key constituents get the chance to see the article. Don't
  leave anything to chance when you land a national placement.
  Take some time to enjoy your success, and then leverage the
  placement for all that it's worth. Enjoy your successes!

Glossary Terms

Advertising -- Messages in a publication, broadcast program or Internet web site that are financially subsidized by an outside organization.

B-roll – Film or videotape that can be used as background during narration of a video news segment intended for broadcast or Internet web cast.

Backgrounder – A document prepared to provide context about an organization's goals, aims, policies, programs or activities.

Buckley Amendment – A law protecting the confidentiality of certain records. In the context of higher education, it restricts colleges and universities from releasing information on students' grades, academic majors and other data to the public without the permission of the students.

Crib sheets – Notes on paper to assist a public relations person with important aspects of a verbal pitch when contacting national reporters.

Development – The euphemism preferred by colleges and universities for describing their fund raising activities.

Editorial – The editorial side of a publication, broadcast outlet or Internet web site is the unit assigned the task of preparing the information for each issue or program. An editorial can also be an article or broadcast that officially articulates the publisher's or station owner's official position on a topic.

Editorial Board Meeting – A meeting held with the members of a publication or broadcast outlet who are responsible for determining the editorial policy of the organization.

Feature Article – A news story that is not tied to a "hard" or "spot" news event of general public interest. Often a story that explains a circumstance or condition in depth.

Feature Story – The same as a feature article.

Five Ws – The essential elements of a standard news story that answers the questions who, what, when, where and why.

Fog Index – A mathematical method used to determine the readability of a passage of text. In general, the higher the fog index, the more difficult the text is to read.

Foundations – Organizations designed to bring aid, usually philanthropic, to a specific cause or concern.

Fund Raising – In the context of this book, the administrative action of nonprofit organizations to secure financial donations for their own well-being.

Hour Glass Format – A writing style in which the prominent news of a story is reported in the first few paragraphs followed by a transitional paragraph that introduces the chronology of events.

Inverted Pyramid Style – A literary device used by journalists to include first the most important facts in a story while putting the least important facts at the end. Doing so ensures that if a story is cut by an editor, the reader will still learn the most important points.

Leads – The beginning of a news story, whether printed or broadcast, is referred to as the lead.

Letters To The Editor –Letters by readers sent to news outlets in reaction to stories that have been printed by the news outlet.

Marketing – The process by which organizations decide which products and services to offer, the prices at which they will be offered, when, where and how they will be offered, and how they will be promoted to appropriate audiences.

Media Coverage – In this context, the stories, articles and news programs produced by news outlets mentioning a specific organization.

Media Relations – The process by which companies, government, non-profit organizations and individuals interact with the news media.

Media Session – Usually a meeting between a senior official for an organization and members of the news media; often conducted at the offices of the news outlet.

Narrative Style – A form of writing used in feature stories which attempts to draw people into a story by placing them in the middle of the action.

News Conference – A meeting to which journalists are invited at a specific time and place, usually to hear an announcement of news from a senior official of an organization and then journalists are given a chace to question that official.

Op/Ed – Opinion articles written, in this context, by persons who are not on the editorial staff of the newspaper or magazine publishing the articles. The term op/ed comes from the typical placement of such articles in newspapers. They usually are placed opposite the editorial page.

Photo Shoot – The process of taking photographs for publication.

Positioning – The activity by which organizations establish a desired place in a market.

PRSA – The Public Relations Society of America.

Press Release – A written announcement of news offered by an organization to news outlets; usually sent to more than one outlet at the same time.

Product Branding – The process by which organizations establish firm awareness of and favorable identification with their product(s) within markets.

Public Relations Department – The administrative unit charged with creating and maintaining favorable relations among the several audiences or "publics" that are important to the organization's success.

Round-Up Story – A news story with sources from several similar organizations. Example: A story on college tuition increases might "round up" comments from spokespersons at five or six schools.

Score – In this context, a favorable mention of an organization in a news story that occurs as a result of public relations activities.

Summary Lead – A first paragraph that summarizes the information to follow in a news story.

Third-Party Endorsement – A favorable testimonial for the organization or its products or services that does not come directly from the organization itself.

Trend Story – A news story citing several sources from similar organizations to establish that an activity, program or idea is part of a growing trend; similar to the roundup story.

Index

Trellis Publishing, Inc.
DIRECT ORDER FORM
HOW TO GET NOTICED BY THE NATIONAL MEDIA:
YOUR COMPLETE GUIDE TO HIGH-IMPACT PUBLICITY

*   Fax orders: 715-399-0781
°   Telephone orders: Call Toll Free: 1 (800) 513-0115.
•   Postal orders: **Trellis Publishing, Inc.**
                   P.O. Box 16141
                   Duluth, MN 55816

Bill and Ship to:

Company Name: _____

Contact Person: _____

Address: _____

City: _____ State: _____ Zip: _____-_____

Daytime telephone: (_____) _____

e-mail_____

Ordering Information:

How To Get National Media Attention	Retail $19.95	Quantity	Price	Total
			Subtotal:	

Quantity Discounts:

Quantity	Discount	Price
3-4	20%	$15.95
5-24	40%	$11.95
25-99	50%	$ 9.95

Shipping:

$1.00 - $20	$ 3.00	
$20.01- $40	$ 4.00	
$40.01- $70	$ 6.00	
$70.01- $120	$ 8.00	
$120.01-$200	$12.00	
Over $200	6% of order	_____

(AZ residents add 7%, WI residents add 6%, MN residents at 6.5%) _____

                      Total Price: _____

Type of Payment:

☐ Cheque enclosed, Payable to: Trellis Publishing, Inc.

Credit Card: ☐ VISA ☐ MASTERCARD ☐ AMERICAN EXPRESS ☐ DISCOVER

Card number:_____

Name on card: _____ Expiration Date:_____ /_____

Signature:_____